W9-AJI-299

3 9077 04552 7572

IT'S A MAGICAL WORLD

Other Books by Bill Watterson

Calvin and Hobbes
Something Under the Bed Is Drooling
Yukon Ho!
Weirdos from Another Planet
The Revenge of the Baby-Sat
Scientific Progress Goes "Boink"
Attack of the Deranged Mutant Killer Monster Snow Goons
The Days Are Just Packed
Homicidal Psycho Jungle Cat
There's Treasure Everywhere

Treasury Collections

The Essential Calvin and Hobbes
The Calvin and Hobbes Lazy Sunday Book
The Authoritative Calvin and Hobbes
The Indispensable Calvin and Hobbes
The Calvin and Hobbes Tenth Anniversary Book

IT'S A MAGICAL WORLD

A Calvin and Hobbes Collection by Bill Watterson

Andrews and McMeel
A Universal Press Syndicate Company
Kansas City

ISBN: 0-8362-2234-2 hardback
0-8362-2136-2 paperback

Library of Congress Catalog Card Number: 96-83996

First Printing, July 1996
Third Printing, November 1996

OOL
Calvin and HOBBES
by WATTERSON
!
ZZZ
ZZZZZZ
OOMF!
CAT NAP, NOUN: A QUICK, LIGHT DOZE IN THE MANNER OF CATS.
I KNOW WHAT IT MEANS!

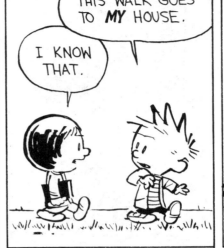

FREE!
HA HA!

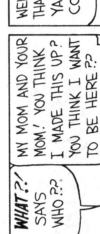

THIS WALK GOES TO **MY** HOUSE.
I KNOW THAT.

YOUR HOUSE IS OVER THERE. WANT ME TO DRAW YOU A MAP OF HOW TO GET THERE?
OBVIOUSLY I'M NOT **GOING** TO MY HOUSE.

IT'S A LOT **MORE** OBVIOUS THAT YOU'RE NOT COMING TO **MY** HOUSE!
I HAVE TO STAY HERE UNTIL MY MOM GETS HOME.

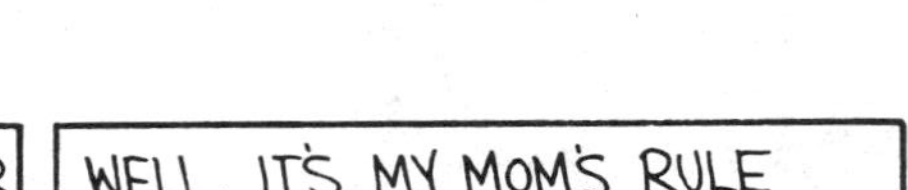
WHAT?! SAYS WHO??
MY MOM AND YOUR MOM! YOU THINK I MADE THIS UP? YOU THINK I WANT TO BE HERE??

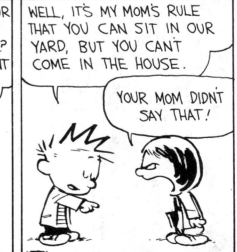

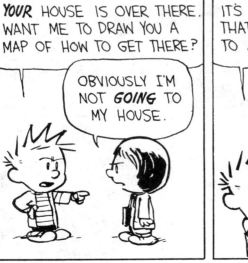

WELL, IT'S MY MOM'S RULE THAT YOU CAN SIT IN OUR YARD, BUT YOU CAN'T COME IN THE HOUSE.
YOUR MOM DIDN'T SAY THAT!

LET ME IN! YOUR MOM SAID I COULD STAY HERE!
NO! GO AWAY! YOU CAN WAIT IN A TREE!

I'M TELLING! HELLO? HELLO? CALVIN WON'T LET ME IN!
AAUGH! SHH! SHHH! OK, OK!

IN FACT, HEH HEH HEH, WHY DON'T YOU GO IN AHEAD OF ME? I JUST REMEMBERED A BIG ORANGE SURPRISE WAITING FOR YOU! DON'T BE SCARED!

YEAH, I'M TREMBLING.
I'LL JUST STEP WAY, WAY BACK HERE!

IS THIS YOUR "BIG ORANGE SURPRISE"?
DOGGONE IT, HOBBES! DIDN'T YOU POUNCE?!

HERE'S YOUR TIGER. HE WAS BY THE DOOR.
WHAT'S WITH THE TIE?!

HELLO, SUSIE. COME ON IN.
MY MOM DIDN'T CALL AND SAY I COULD GO HOME YET, DID SHE?
YOU DRESSED UP FOR A GIRL???!

WOULD YOU CARE FOR A SNACK, SUSIE?
UM, OK. THANK YOU.
WELL? WHAT HAVE YOU GOT TO SAY FOR YOURSELF?
WHEN ONE ENTERTAINS FEMALE FRIENDS, ONE SHOULD TRY NOT TO LOOK QUITE AS SEEDY AS CERTAIN UNNAMED PARTIES HABITUALLY DO.
WHO'S ENTERTAINING?! WHO'S A FEMALE FRIEND? WHO LOOKS SEEDY?!
A SPOTTED TIE IS JUST THE THING WHEN YOU'RE WEARING STRIPES! TIGERS HAVE A NATURAL FLAIR FOR CASUAL CHIC!
I CAN'T BELIEVE THIS! WHY DIDN'T YOU KILL HER WHEN SHE CAME IN THE DOOR?!
BY THE WAY, IF YOU HAD MADE PROPER INTRODUCTIONS, WE MIGHT HAVE SMOOCHED HER HAND.
HERE, LET ME ADJUST THE NARROW END OF YOUR TIE ABOUT EIGHT INCHES.

WHAT HAPPENED TO **YOU**?
HOBBES AND I HAD A FRANK EXCHANGE OF IDEAS.
WHAT ARE YOU DOING? HOMEWORK??
I WASN'T SURE I UNDERSTOOD THIS CHAPTER, SO I REVIEWED MY NOTES FROM THE LAST CHAPTER AND NOW I'M REREADING THIS.
YOU DO ALL THAT **WORK**?!
WELL, NOW I UNDERSTAND IT.
HUH! I USED TO THINK YOU WERE SMART.

WHERE'S SUSIE?
SHE'S IN THE LIVING ROOM DOING HER HOMEWORK!

NOW? SHE'S NOT PUTTING IT OFF UNTIL BEDTIME?
SHE SAYS SHE NEEDS TO GET IT DONE SO SHE CAN PRACTICE THE PIANO WHEN SHE GOES HOME!

WOW, IT'S LIKE SCIENCE FICTION OR SOMETHING.
"THE GENDER FROM OUTER SPACE"!
WATTERSON

THIS EMERGENCY MEETING OF THE GET RID OF SLIMY GIRLS CLUB WILL COME TO ORDER, DICTATOR-FOR-LIFE CALVIN PRESIDING!
OYEZ! OYEZ!
G.R.O.S.S.

AS WE'RE ALL AWARE, THE ENEMY HAS INFILTRATED OUR TERRITORY AND IS SPREADING DISINFORMATION TO THE EFFECT THAT HOMEWORK OUGHT TO BE DONE RIGHT AFTER SCHOOL!

AS MY MOM MAY HAVE COVERT GIRL SYMPATHIES, WE MUST ERADICATE THE HOSTILE FORCES! ANY QUESTIONS?

YES, COULD WE POKE SOME AIR HOLES IN HERE?
TOO RISKY. THE BOX OF SECRECY MUST REMAIN SECURE!
G.R.O.S.S.
WATTERSON

OK, WE BOTH UNDERSTAND THE SECRET PLAN?
GOT IT. BUT WHAT ABOUT A SECRET CODE?
A SECRET CODE? THIS SECRET PLAN DOESN'T NEED A SECRET CODE.
AHEM.
"SECTION IV, ARTICLE 12: EVERY SECRET PLAN NEEDS A SECRET CODE.
A. THE MORE COMPLICATED, THE BETTER.
B. EVERYBODY ALREADY KNOWS PIG LATIN.
C. PHRASES LIKE 'CODE BLUE' ARE COOL."
OUR CLUB CHARTER NEVER LIES.
THAT'S WHY THIS IS SUCH A GREAT CLUB.

HEY! I CAN'T GET OUT! I'M STUCK! HELP!
CALVIN?
SUSIE, I'M TRAPPED IN THE HALL CLOSET! OPEN THE DOOR! LET ME OUT! HELP! HELP!
HURRY! QUICK! I'M IN THE CLOSET! OPEN THE DOOR AND GET ME OUT OF...
SLAM
HEY!
YES!

CALVIN, ARE YOU SLAMMING DOORS?!
IT WASN'T ME, MOM! I DIDN'T HEAR ANYTHING!

LET ME OUT OF HERE, CALVIN, YOU ROTTEN BAG OF BARF!
WHEEE! OUR CLUB'S FINEST HOUR!

WHERE'S SUSIE?
BEATS ME. MAYBE SHE WENT OUTSIDE.
I'M IN HERE! LET ME OUT!

WHY, SUSIE! WHAT WERE YOU DOING IN THE CLOSET, OF ALL PLACES?
CALVIN.....
HE TRICKED ME IN THERE AND HELD THE DOOR!

SUSIE, YOUR MOM JUST CALLED AND SHE'S WALKING OVER TO PICK YOU UP.
FINALLY!

I'LL TALK TO YOU IN A FEW MINUTES, UPSTAIRS.
BYE SUSIE! DON'T LOCK YOURSELF IN ANY MORE CLOSETS!

WE GOT RID OF A SLIMY GIRL! WHAT A GREAT DAY OF GROSSNESS!
THIS GOES IN THE LOG BOOK!

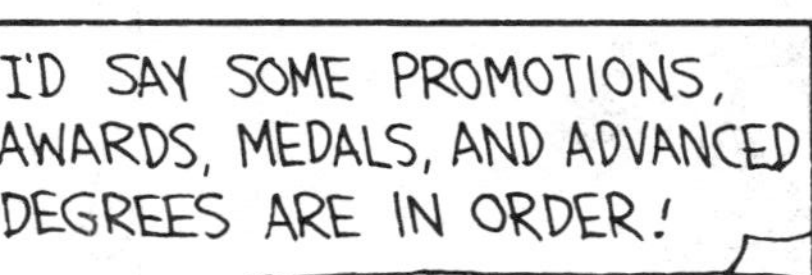

I'D SAY SOME PROMOTIONS, AWARDS, MEDALS, AND ADVANCED DEGREES ARE IN ORDER!
SHOULD WE GET THEM BEFORE WE GET IN TROUBLE, OR AFTER?

calvin and HOBBES by WATTERSON

THE SECRET TO ENJOYING YOUR JOB IS TO HAVE A HOBBY THAT'S EVEN WORSE.

What was the significance of the Erie Canal?

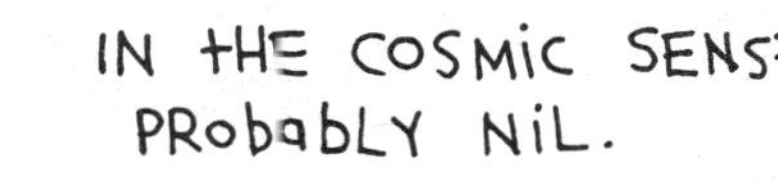

IN THE COSMIC SENSE, PRObabLY NIL.

WE "BIG PICTURE" PEOPLE RARELY BECOME HISTORIANS.

REMEMBER WHEN I WAS FIRST BORN? I COULDN'T EVEN TURN MYSELF OVER! MY EYES WOULDN'T FOCUS! I COULDN'T DO ANYTHING!

THINK OF ALL THE WORK IT TOOK TO DEVELOP THE MOTOR SKILLS NECESSARY TO HOLD A CRAYON, TO PLACE THE TIP OF IT ON A PAGE, AND TO MOVE IT IN PREDETERMINED, COORDINATED MOTIONS!

THIS PICTURE IS THE RESULT OF SIX YEARS' UNRELENTING TOIL! A LIFETIME OF EFFORT WENT INTO THIS!

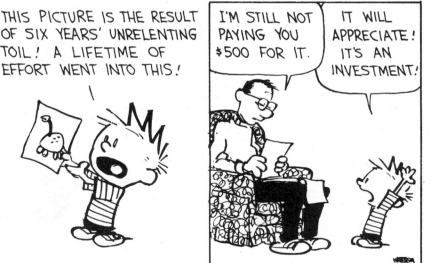

I'M STILL NOT PAYING YOU $500 FOR IT.
IT WILL APPRECIATE! IT'S AN INVESTMENT!

CALVIN?
CALVIN!
CALVIN!
AAUGH!!
SORRY. MY EYES WERE ON SCREEN SAVER.

RIGHT HERE! PUT IT HERE!
AAAA!!
521
LET'S WORK ON YOUR UNDERHAND PITCHES.
IF YOU KEEP RUNNING AWAY LIKE THAT, YOU WON'T CATCH ANY FOULS.

GET GOING, OR YOU'LL MISS THE SCHOOL BUS.
calvin and HOBBES
by WATTERSON
UH... GREETINGS. MY NAME IS CALVIN.
POOF
GRITTINGS. MA NAM IS KAHLFIN.
GRITTINGS. MA NAM IS KAHLFIN.
UM..YES! WELL CALVIN, HERE'S YOUR LUNCHBOX. HAVE A GOOD DAY AT SCHOOL.
HOFFA GUD TAY.
LUNBOKS.
HI CALVIN.
GRITTINGS. MA NAM IS KAHLFIN. HEERYOR LUNBOKS. HOFFA GUD TAY ASKOOL.
CALVIN'S PRINCIPAL SAYS TO SAY HELLO.
HUH BOY.
IT TROO! DAT DARN KAHLFIN STOLE MA SPACECHIP!

CALVIN, ARE YOU CHEWING GUM IN CLASS?
YETH.
DO YOU HAVE ENOUGH TO SHARE WITH EVERYBODY?
PROBABLY, BUT DO YOU REALLY THINK THEY'D WANT IT??
IT WAS **HER** IDEA...

AHEM.
HI.

WHAT'S THE POINT OF WEARING YOUR FAVORITE ROCKETSHIP UNDERPANTS IF NOBODY EVER ASKS TO SEE 'EM?

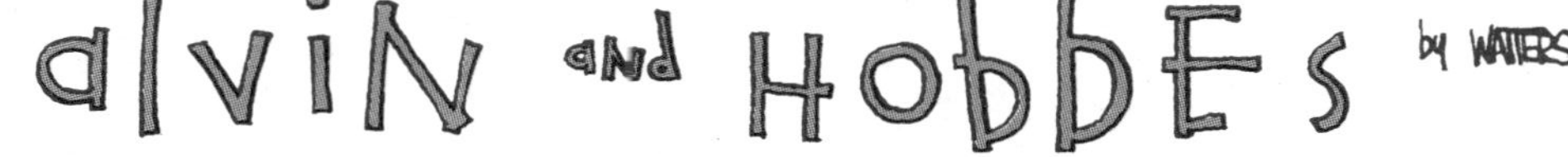

AH, WHAT A LOVELY DAY TO GO SAILING, EH MARSHA?
OUR NEW BOAT IS JUST WONDERFUL, BRADLEY.

WHAT DO YOU SAY WE DROP ANCHOR AND GO FOR A SWIM, DEAREST?
THAT SOUNDS DELIGHTFUL, DARLING! LET'S GO!

PLOOSH PLOOSH

AAA!! AAA!! THIS LAKE IS BOILING HOT! WE'RE GETTING SCALDED!! GET OUT OF THE WATER! AA! OW! AA! OW!

I'VE GOT SECOND DEGREE BURNS ALL OVER! WHAT KIND OF LAKE *IS* THIS?!
WE NEED MEDICAL ATTENTION, BRADLEY! PULL UP THE ANCHOR!

BRADLEY, WE'RE GOING THE WRONG WAY!
I CAN'T HELP IT, MARSHA! THE WIND IS BLOWING US OVER HERE, TOWARD THE... THE...

THE WATERFALL! OH NO! AAAAA! BLUB BLUB! AAAA! GLUB GLUB GLUB!

HELP, HELP! THE WIND IS PICKING UP AGAIN! HANG ON! WE'RE FLYING RIGHT OUT OF THE WATER!
DON'T LOOK DOWN, MARSHA! WE'RE MILES HIGH!

UH OH! THE WIND SUDDENLY STOPPED!!
AAAAAAA AAAAA AAAAAAAA

WE.. WE'RE ALIVE! WE SOMEHOW LANDED IN ANOTHER LAKE! BUT WHERE *ARE* WE?!
I HAVE A BAD FEELING ABOUT THIS, BRADLEY.

IT'S A GIGANTIC WHIRLPOOL!! WE'RE GOING DOWN! WAAAAAA!!

HERE'S THE PROBLEM. THAT'LL BE $150.
SOMEBODY *ELSE* IS GOING TO PAY FOR THIS TOO.

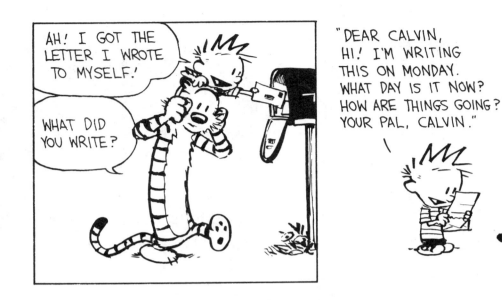

AH! I GOT THE LETTER I WROTE TO MYSELF!
WHAT DID YOU WRITE?

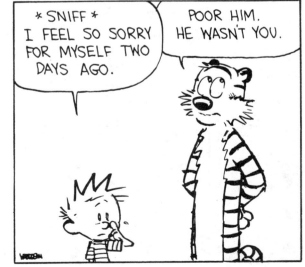

"DEAR CALVIN,
HI! I'M WRITING THIS ON MONDAY.
WHAT DAY IS IT NOW?
HOW ARE THINGS GOING?
YOUR PAL, CALVIN."

MY PAST SELF IS CORRESPONDING WITH MY FUTURE SELF.
TOO BAD YOU CAN'T WRITE BACK.

I GOT ANOTHER LETTER FROM MY PAST SELF.
WHAT'S IT SAY?

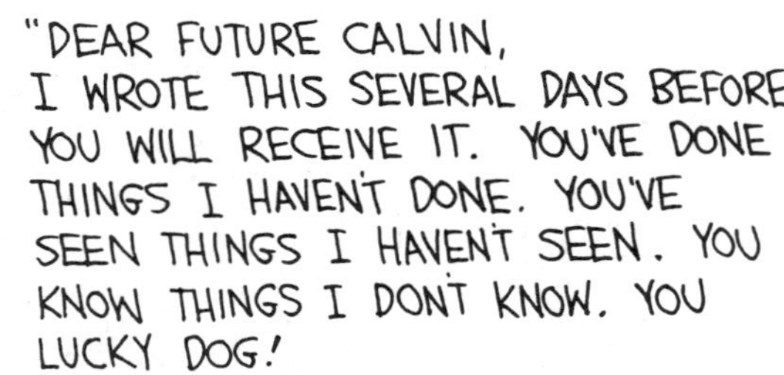
"DEAR FUTURE CALVIN,
I WROTE THIS SEVERAL DAYS BEFORE YOU WILL RECEIVE IT. YOU'VE DONE THINGS I HAVEN'T DONE. YOU'VE SEEN THINGS I HAVEN'T SEEN. YOU KNOW THINGS I DON'T KNOW. YOU LUCKY DOG!
YOUR PAL,
CALVIN."

SNIFF I FEEL SO SORRY FOR MYSELF TWO DAYS AGO.
POOR HIM. HE WASN'T YOU.

I THINK I SHOULD STAY HOME FROM SCHOOL. I'VE GOT A SORE THROAT, AN EAR ACHE, A STOMACH ACHE, I'M SEEING SPOTS, AND I'M DIZZY.
I'LL CALL THE DOCTOR.
HOLD ON, I THINK IT'S ALL CLEARING UP! YES, I THINK I'M BETTER NOW.
IT'S PRETTY HARD TO HIT THAT MAGIC NUMBER OF APPROPRIATELY VAGUE, MILDLY SERIOUS, BUT NOT QUITE WORRISOME SYMPTOMS.

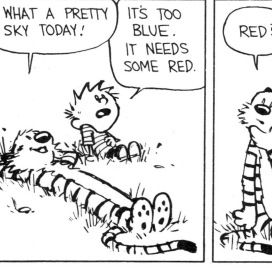

WHAT A PRETTY SKY TODAY!
IT'S TOO BLUE. IT NEEDS SOME RED.
RED?
JUST A LITTLE, RIGHT OVER THERE.
HANG ON.
THAT'S BETTER.
WELL I'LL BE!

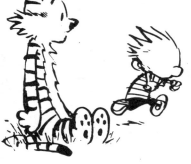

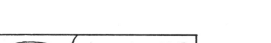

LET'S DRAW THE LINE AT THE UMBRELLA.

I HATE ALL THIS WIND! BOY, THIS IS UNPLEASANT! STUPID, MISERABLE WIND! WHAT LOUSY WEATHER! WHAT AN AWFUL DAY!
WELL IF YOU CAN'T CHANGE IT, WHAT'S THE POINT IN GRIPING ABOUT IT?
I'M NOT GOING TO LET A LITTLE WIND BE MORE ANNOYING THAN ME.

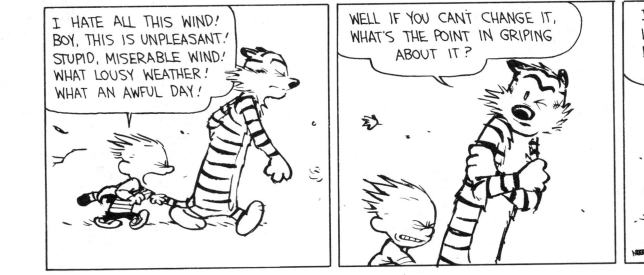

LOOK AT ALL THE STARS! THE UNIVERSE JUST GOES OUT FOREVER AND EVER!

IT KIND OF MAKES YOU WONDER WHY MAN CONSIDERS HIMSELF SUCH A BIG SCREAMING DEAL.
CALVIN AND HOBBES by WATTERSON
THAT'S WHY WE STAY INSIDE WITH OUR APPLIANCES.

THIS NEW ISSUE OF *CHEWING* MAGAZINE TELLS HOW TO SET UP A MANDIBULAR FITNESS REGIME!
WATTERSON

BASICALLY, THEY RECOMMEND INTERVAL TRAINING: CHEWING ONE PIECE OF GUM WITH LOTS OF REPS, FOLLOWED BY CHEWING FIVE PIECES OF GUM AT ONCE, SO YOU REALLY WORK THE MASSETER AND BUCCINATOR MUSCLES.
IT'S A GRUELING WORKOUT, BUT YOU BUILD STRENGTH **AND** ENDURANCE, SO YOU CAN COME THROUGH IN A CLINCHER.
I'M SURE THE GLORY MAKES IT ALL WORTHWHILE.
PLUS, YOU DEVELOP THAT "CHEWER'S JAW" THAT DRIVES THE GIRLS WILD.
WHAT'S WITH THE FACE?
I'M DOING STRETCHES.
WATTERSON
CHEWING MAGAZINE SAYS YOU SHOULD ALWAYS WARM UP BEFORE YOU CHEW GUM.
DID YOU KNOW THAT NEGLECTING TO STRETCH THE TEMPORALIS MUSCLES IS THE LEADING CAUSE OF GUM CHEWING INJURIES?

WHAT ABOUT FALLING DOWN WHILE CHEWING AND WALKING?
WITH A GOOD HELMET, THE RISK IS SURPRISINGLY SMALL.

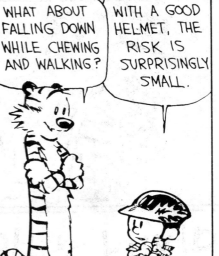

IN THIS ISSUE, CHEWING REVIEWS THE NEW GUM CHEWING APPAREL.

THIS JERSEY IS MADE WITH SWET-TEK® FIBERS THAT WICK AWAY PERSPIRATION! THE MESH COLLAR KEEPS YOUR STERNOMASTOIDS VENTILATED AND THE ZIPPERED POCKETS HOLD SPARE GUM AND WRAPPERS!

WHY IS IT COVERED WITH BRAND LOGOS?
THAT GIVES YOU THE PSYCHOLOGICAL EDGE OF PRETENDING YOU'RE SPONSORED.

HOW CAN YOU TELL IF YOU'RE READING AN ADVERTISEMENT, A PRODUCT REVIEW, OR THE PRODUCT ITSELF?
I'D SURE LIKE TO BE A WALKING ENDORSEMENT.

I NEED TO GET A HEART RATE MONITOR.

WHAT FOR?

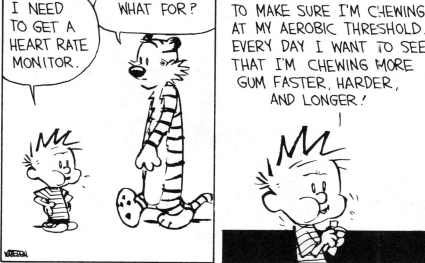

TO MAKE SURE I'M CHEWING AT MY AEROBIC THRESHOLD! EVERY DAY I WANT TO SEE THAT I'M CHEWING MORE GUM FASTER, HARDER, AND LONGER!

WHAT'S THE POINT OF ATTACHING A NUMBER TO EVERYTHING YOU DO?

IF YOUR NUMBERS GO UP, IT MEANS YOU'RE HAVING MORE FUN.
SCIENCE TO THE SPIRIT'S RESCUE ONCE AGAIN.

WHAT ON EARTH AM I DOING IN HERE ON THIS BEAUTIFUL DAY?!
THIS IS THE ONLY LIFE I'VE GOT!!

AAAAAAAAAA

NEXT TIME, TRY A DRINK OF WATER AND A FEW DEEP BREATHS.

LOOK! A TRICKLE OF WATER RUNNING THROUGH SOME DIRT!

I'D SAY OUR AFTERNOON JUST GOT BOOKED SOLID!

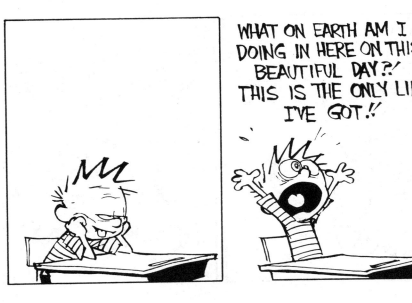

Calvin and Hobbes by Watterson

I SUPPOSE THE SECRET TO HAPPINESS IS LEARNING TO APPRECIATE THE MOMENT.
I, FOR EXAMPLE, TAKE GREAT PLEASURE IN BEING RIGHT HERE, RIGHT NOW, DOING WHAT WE'RE DOING.
OF COURSE, YOU'RE SUPPOSED TO BE AT SCHOOL.
I COULDN'T APPRECIATE THOSE MOMENTS.

WHY AREN'T WE HOOKED UP TO AN ON-LINE SERVICE, SO WE CAN CONNECT TO OTHER COMPUTERS?
BECAUSE IT'S BAD ENOUGH WE HAVE A TELEPHONE.
HELLLPPP!!

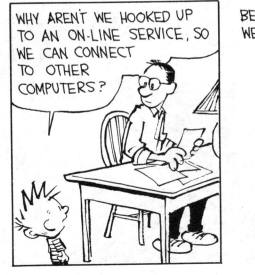

I HATE WHEN A LOT OF KIDS ARE ON THE SLIDE. YOU WAIT FOREVER TO GET TO THE TOP AND THEN THE RIDE IS OVER SO FAST.
AND IF YOU SIT FOR A MOMENT TO ENJOY THE HEIGHT, EVERYBODY YELLS AT YOU TO GET GOING.
AND SOMETIMES THE IDIOT BEHIND YOU STARTS DOWN TOO SOON AND HE SMACKS INTO YOU AT THE BOTTOM BEFORE YOU CAN GET AWAY.

YEP, THE PLAYGROUND IS A **LOT** MORE FUN AFTER CLASS STARTS.
CALVIN!
WATTERSON

PHOOMPP
WHY ARE YOU CRYING?
I'M CUTTING UP AN ONION.
IT MUST BE HARD TO COOK IF YOU ANTHROPOMORPHIZE YOUR VEGETABLES.
WATTERSON

CALVIN, WOULD YOU DEMONSTRATE THE NEXT PROBLEM AT THE BOARD?
YES MISS WORM-WOOD. I WOULD BE HAP-PY TO DO AN-Y-THING YOU ASK.

I HAVE BEEN SUC-CESS-FUL-LY PRO-GRAMMED TO OBEY ALL DI-REC-TIVES. I HAVE NO WILL OF MY OWN... MY OWN MY OWN... MY OWN.

DOESN'T ANYBODY APPRECIATE THEATER ?!
NCIPAL

CAN I RUN THE VACUUM CLEANER?
NO, NOT UNTIL YOU'RE OLDER.
I'M OLD ENOUGH! I COULD DO IT!
WELL, MAYBE JUST THIS ONCE, IF YOU DO A REAL GOOD JOB.

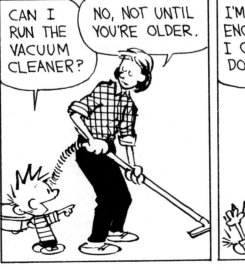

THAT SUPPRESSED SMILE WORRIES ME.

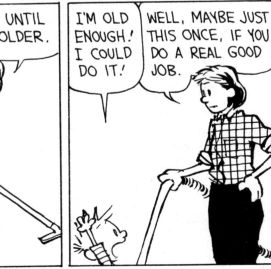

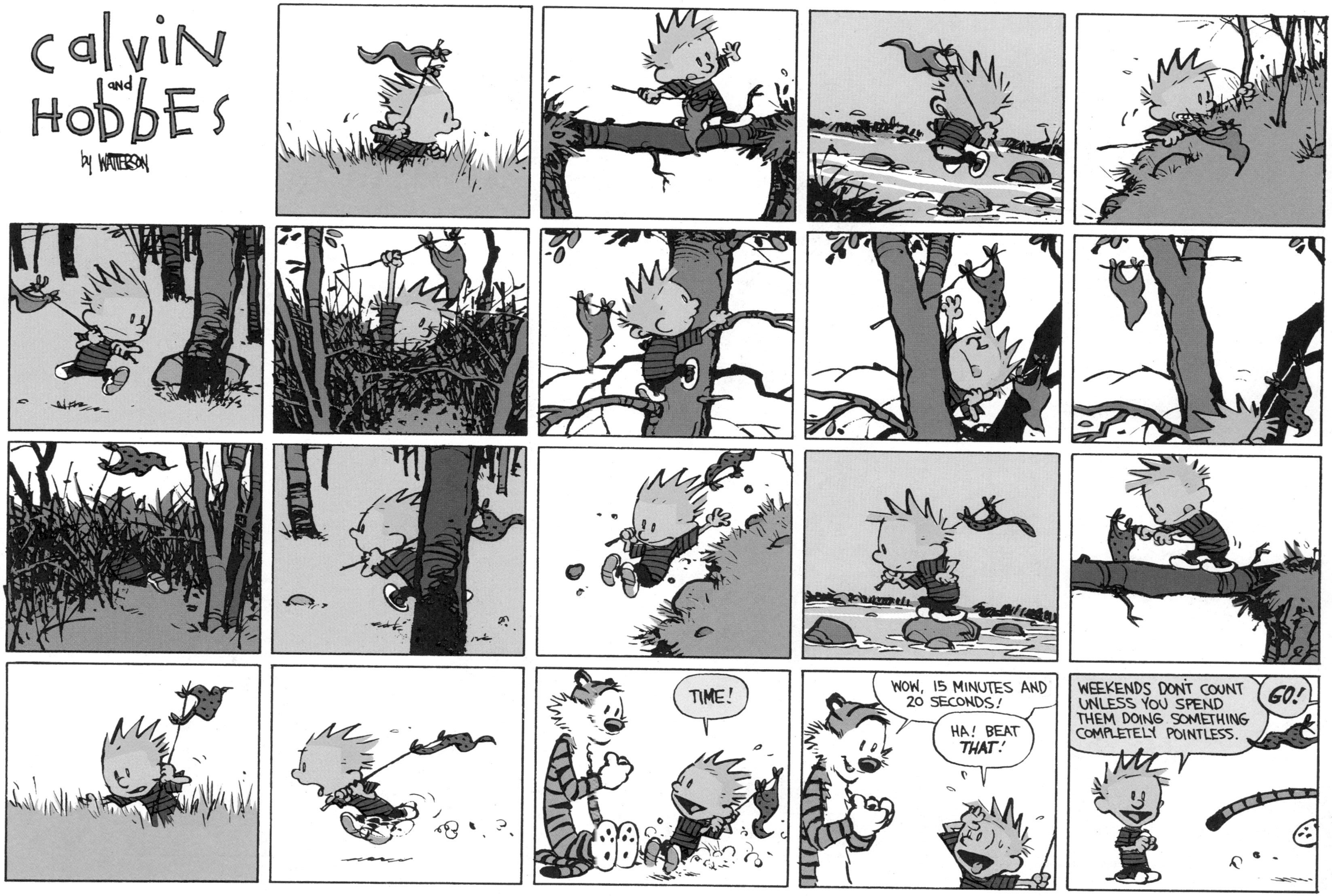

Calvin and Hobbes

by WATTERSON

TIME!

WOW, 15 MINUTES AND 20 SECONDS!

HA! BEAT THAT!

WEEKENDS DON'T COUNT UNLESS YOU SPEND THEM DOING SOMETHING COMPLETELY POINTLESS.

GO!

"PLEASE EXCUSE CALVIN FROM CLASS TODAY. HIS GENIUS IS URGENTLY REQUIRED ON A TOP SECRET MATTER OF NATIONAL SECURITY. SINCERELY, THE PRESIDENT OF THE UNITED STATES. P.S. REALLY."

NICE TRY. SIT DOWN.

I GOTTA LEARN HOW TO WRITE IN CURSIVE.

HOW COME GROWN-UPS DON'T GO OUT TO PLAY?

GROWN-UPS CAN ONLY JUSTIFY PLAYING OUTSIDE BY CALLING IT EXERCISE, DOING IT WHEN THEY'D RATHER NOT, AND KEEPING RECORDS TO QUANTIFY THEIR PERFORMANCE.

THAT SOUNDS LIKE A JOB.
..EXCEPT YOU DON'T GET PAID.

SO PLAY IS WORSE THAN WORK?
BEING A GROWN-UP IS TOUGH.

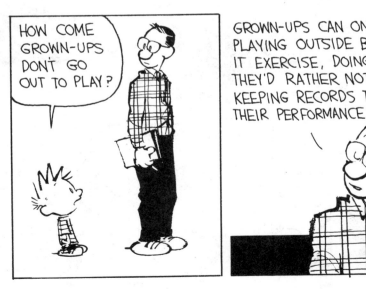

A BIG PART OF LIFE IS BORING ROUTINE. I NEED MORE EXCITEMENT.

SO TODAY, I'M GOING TO HAVE A NEW KIND OF CEREAL!

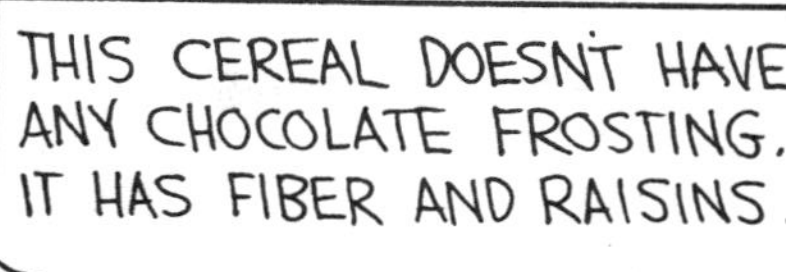

THIS CEREAL DOESN'T HAVE ANY CHOCOLATE FROSTING. IT HAS FIBER AND RAISINS.
PULP 'N' STUFF

OF COURSE, A BIG PART OF LIFE IS HORRIFYING SURPRISE. ROUTINES CAN BE COMFORTING.
WE TIGERS PREFER TO INFLICT EXCITEMENT ON OTHERS.

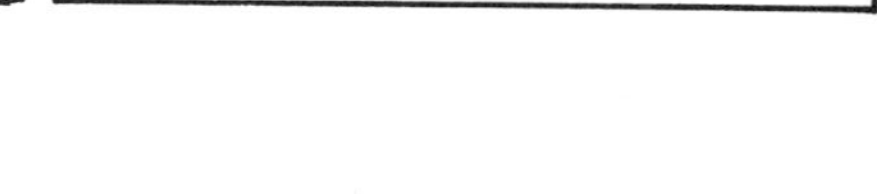

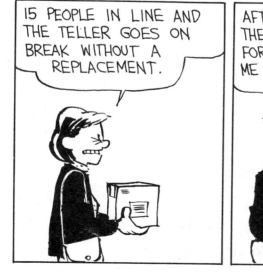

15 PEOPLE IN LINE AND THE TELLER GOES ON BREAK WITHOUT A REPLACEMENT.

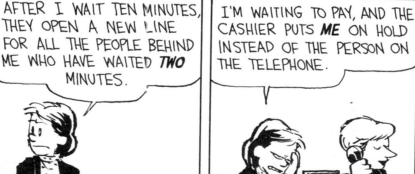

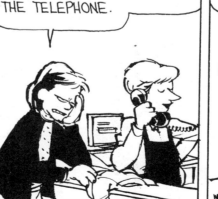

AFTER I WAIT TEN MINUTES, THEY OPEN A NEW LINE FOR ALL THE PEOPLE BEHIND ME WHO HAVE WAITED **TWO** MINUTES.

I'M WAITING TO PAY, AND THE CASHIER PUTS **ME** ON HOLD INSTEAD OF THE PERSON ON THE TELEPHONE.

HAVE A NICE DAY.
TOO LATE.

HAVE YOU NOTICED HOW NOBODY DRESSES UP FOR ANYTHING ANYMORE? PEOPLE LOOK LIKE SLOBS EVERYWHERE THEY GO.

EVERYBODY'S RUDE, TOO. PEOPLE SWEAR ALL THE TIME, AND YOU CAN FORGET ABOUT BEING ADDRESSED AS "MR." OR "SIR." THERE'S NO RESPECT FOR ANYONE.

HOW COME *I* GOTTA CHANGE THE WORLD ?!
WATTERSON

EVERY SATURDAY MORNING IS THE SAME.

WE GET UP AT THE CRACK OF DAWN, WATCH CARTOONS AND EAT SUGARY CEREAL UNTIL WE FIGHT, AND THEN MOM THROWS US OUT OF THE HOUSE. IT NEVER CHANGES.
THAT'S WHAT *I* LIKE ABOUT SATURDAYS TOO!
FIRST ONE DOWNSTAIRS GETS TO PICK THE CARTOONS!
WATTERSON

Calvin and Hobbes by Watterson

Show and Tell

YOU KNOW, HOBBES, SOME DAYS EVEN MY LUCKY ROCKETSHIP UNDERPANTS DON'T HELP.

WELL, YOU'VE DONE ALL YOU CAN DO.

WHACK

AAA!!
UNG!
RRG!
GRFF!

WHAT ARE YOU SCARED OF? THE BALL'S NOT GOING TO BITE YOU.
HOW DO **YOU** KNOW?

AA!

AA! AA! AA!
MMF!
CHOMP!
RRF!

WHAT DO YOU MEAN, YOU WANT A GLOVE FOR THE OTHER HAND TOO?
WHICH WORD DON'T YOU UNDERSTAND?

Calvin and Hobbes

by WATTERSON

Show and Tell
YOU KNOW, HOBBES, SOME DAYS EVEN MY LUCKY ROCKETSHIP UNDERPANTS DON'T HELP.
WELL, YOU'VE DONE ALL YOU CAN DO.

WHACK

AAA!!
UNG!
RRG!
GRFF!

WHAT ARE YOU SCARED OF? THE BALL'S NOT GOING TO BITE YOU.
HOW DO **YOU** KNOW?

AA!

AA! AA! AA!
MMF!
CHOMP!
RRF!

WHAT DO YOU MEAN, YOU WANT A GLOVE FOR THE OTHER HAND TOO?
WHICH WORD DON'T YOU UNDERSTAND?

AAA!
CLOMP!

HOW OFTEN HAVE I TOLD CALVIN NOT TO LEAVE HIS STUFF IN THE YARD?!

HAVE YOU BEEN HITTING ROCKS WITH THIS BAT?
NO, WHY?
LOOK AT IT. IT'S CHEWED UP. YOU SHOULD TAKE CARE OF YOUR EQUIPMENT.
THE BALL DID THIS!
IT'S WHAT I'VE BEEN TRYING TO TELL YOU! THESE ARE FANG MARKS! THAT BALL IS BERSERK! IT'S DERANGED! IT'S A MENACE!

WHY DO I EVEN BOTHER?

PHOOOOFF

WOW! LOOK AT THE SIZE OF THAT ONE!

BIP

SECRETLY, I WAS HOPING FOR A DEAFENING EXPLOSION.
WATTERSON

FFOOOOFF

FFOOOOF

BIP
WATTERSON

Calvin and Hobbes
by WATTERSON
..YAWWNN...
NYUP NYUP
OOMP!
WAAAAAAAAAAAAAAA
LET GO OF ME, YOU MALEVOLENT, MURDEROUS MORON!!
IT'S MORNING! NOW WE CAN DO STUFF AGAIN!
C'MON! WHEEE!
IT'S HARD TO BE MAD AT SOMEONE WHO MISSES YOU WHILE YOU'RE ASLEEP.

AACKKK

CH... CH... CH...

.. CHOCOLATE CH-CHIPS ..
NO.

AND GET UP OFF THE FLOOR.
URGLE

I'M A GREAT BELIEVER IN THE VALUE OF NOVELTY.

I SAY ANYTHING **NEW** IS **GOOD** BY DEFINITION! IT CAN SHOCK, INSULT, OR OFFEND ME, SO LONG AS IT DOESN'T BORE ME!

IF YOU CAN'T GIVE ME SOMETHING NEW, THEN REPACKAGE THE OLD SO IT ***LOOKS*** NEW! NOVELTY IS ALL THAT MATTERS! I WON'T PAY ATTENTION IF IT'S NOT FRESH AND DIFFERENT!

I SEE WHY TIMELESS TRUTH DOESN'T SELL.
GIVE ME A GOOD FLASH IN THE PAN ANY DAY.

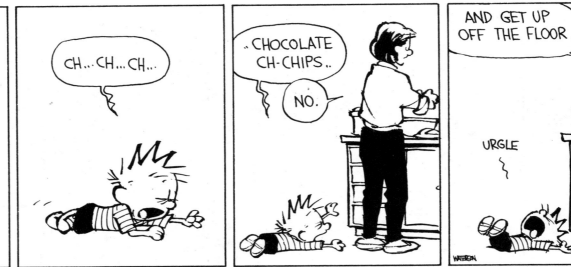

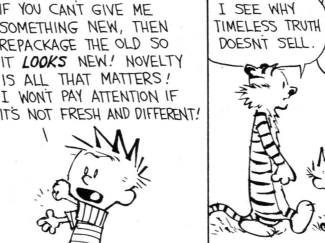

ONE OF US SHOULD HAVE LEFT THE ROOM.

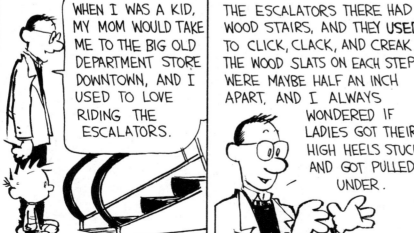

WHEN I WAS A KID, MY MOM WOULD TAKE ME TO THE BIG OLD DEPARTMENT STORE DOWNTOWN, AND I USED TO LOVE RIDING THE ESCALATORS.

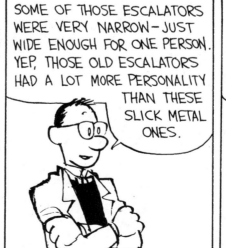

THE ESCALATORS THERE HAD WOOD STAIRS, AND THEY USED TO CLICK, CLACK, AND CREAK. THE WOOD SLATS ON EACH STEP WERE MAYBE HALF AN INCH APART, AND I ALWAYS WONDERED IF LADIES GOT THEIR HIGH HEELS STUCK AND GOT PULLED UNDER.

SOME OF THOSE ESCALATORS WERE VERY NARROW—JUST WIDE ENOUGH FOR ONE PERSON. YEP, THOSE OLD ESCALATORS HAD A LOT MORE PERSONALITY THAN THESE SLICK METAL ONES.

I'D HATE TO THINK THAT ALL MY CURRENT EXPERIENCES WILL SOMEDAY BECOME STORIES WITH NO POINT.

MMF

RRGG

ONE!

REWARD, PLEASE!

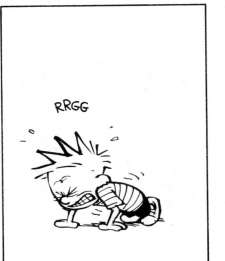

GETTING IS BETTER THAN HAVING.

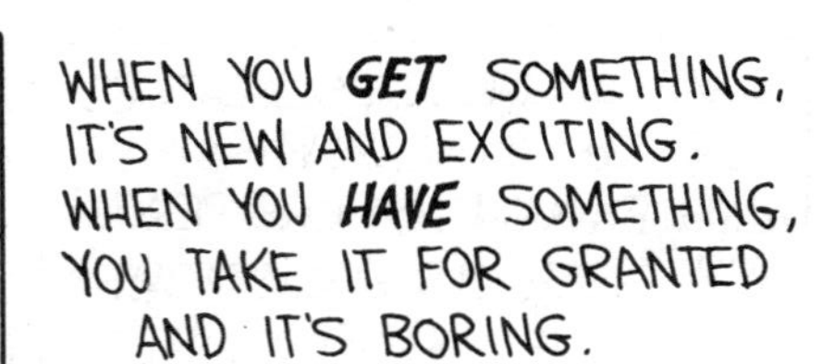
WHEN YOU **GET** SOMETHING, IT'S NEW AND EXCITING. WHEN YOU **HAVE** SOMETHING, YOU TAKE IT FOR GRANTED AND IT'S BORING.

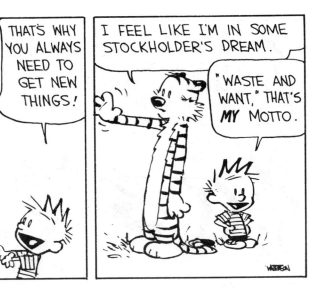

BUT EVERYTHING YOU **GET** TURNS INTO SOMETHING YOU **HAVE**.
THAT'S WHY YOU ALWAYS NEED TO GET NEW THINGS!
I FEEL LIKE I'M IN SOME STOCKHOLDER'S DREAM.
"WASTE AND WANT," THAT'S **MY** MOTTO.

Calvin and Hobbes by Watterson

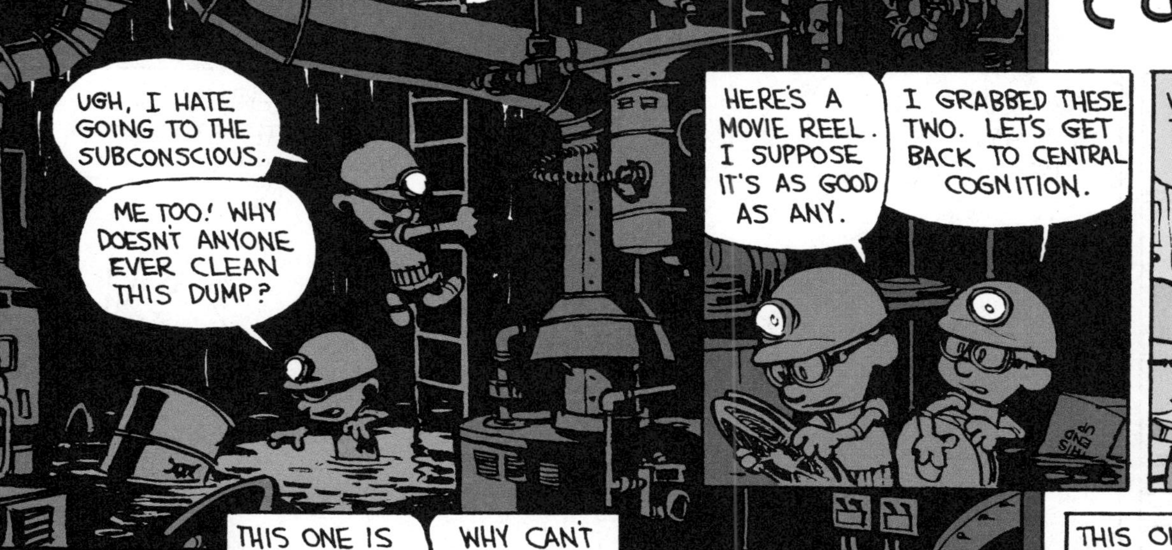

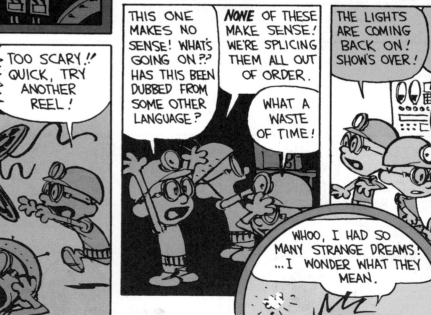

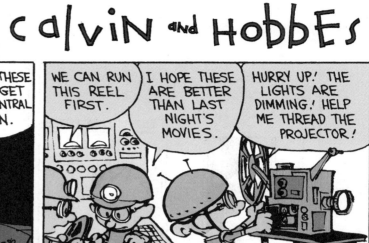

I HEARD THAT MISS WORMWOOD ISN'T HERE TODAY.
REALLY? CAN WE GO HOME?
OF COURSE NOT. WE HAVE A SUBSTITUTE TEACHER.
CAN I SEND IN A SUBSTITUTE STUDENT?

WHO'S OUR SUBSTITUTE TEACHER? DO YOU KNOW?
MR. KNEECAPPER.
OH NO! REALLY? I HEARD HE KILLED A KID LAST YEAR!
WHAT?!
YEAH, SOME KID WAS TALKING IN CLASS, SO MR. KNEECAPPER TOOK HIM OUT IN THE HALL AND THERE WERE STRANGE LUMPS IN THE CAFETERIA MEATLOAF THAT AFTERNOON!
OHH!
WAIT TILL SHE SEES WHAT'S ON TODAY'S LUNCH MENU.

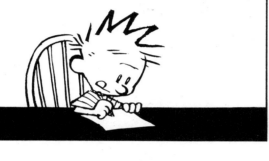

THINGS I WILL NEVER LIKE:
1. DRYING OFF WITH A COLD, DAMP TOWEL.
2. THE FEELING OF SEAWEED WRAPPING AROUND MY LEG.

3. ANYTHING THAT WAS POPULAR IN THE '70s.
4. LICORICE, YAMS, OR RAISINS.
5. THAT HIGH-PITCHED SCREECH THAT BABIES MAKE.
6. WRITHING MAGGOTS.

IT'S COMFORTING TO KNOW THAT THERE ARE CERTAINTIES IN LIFE.

LIFE IS FULL OF POSSIBILITIES.

FOR EXAMPLE, RIGHT NOW, INSTEAD OF WAITING FOR THE SCHOOL BUS, I COULD STICK OUT MY THUMB, HITCH A RIDE, AND SPEND THE REST OF MY LIFE IN THE SERENGETI, MIGRATING WITH THE WILDEBEESTS!

THE SERENGETI IS IN AFRICA. YOU COULDN'T REALLY HITCH A RIDE THERE.

LIFE IS FULL OF PRECLUDED POSSIBILITIES.

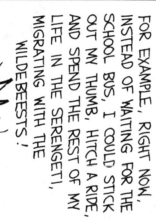

SLURRPP
SLUURRP
AACKKPTH
URGK
BLUB
I'D BET ANYTHING THAT THE PRINCIPAL HAS A VALVE IN HIS OFFICE THAT CHANGES THE WATER PRESSURE.

WHY ARE YOU DIGGING A HOLE?
I'M LOOKING FOR BURIED TREASURE!
WHAT HAVE YOU FOUND?
A FEW DIRTY ROCKS, A WEIRD ROOT, AND SOME DISGUSTING GRUBS.
ON YOUR FIRST TRY??
THERE'S TREASURE EVERYWHERE!

Calvin and Hobbes by WATTERSON
THE FEARLESS SPACEMAN SPIFF, INTERPLANETARY EXPLORER EXTRAORDINAIRE, GAZES ACROSS THE FORBIDDING LANDSCAPE OF AN UNCHARTED PLANET!

WHAT DANGERS LIE AHEAD FOR OUR HERO? WHAT HORRIBLE ALIENS INHABIT THIS WORLD?

WHAT STRANGE ADVENTURES AWAIT THE INTREPID SPIFF? WHAT BIZARRE OCCURRENCE WILL OUR HERO BE THE FIRST TO WITNESS?

THE SUSPENSE!
...OUR HERO CHUCKS A FEW ROCKS..

..SIGHHH...

IF YOU COULDN'T FIND ANY WEIRDNESS, MAYBE WE'LL JUST HAVE TO MAKE SOME!
NOW YER TALKIN'!

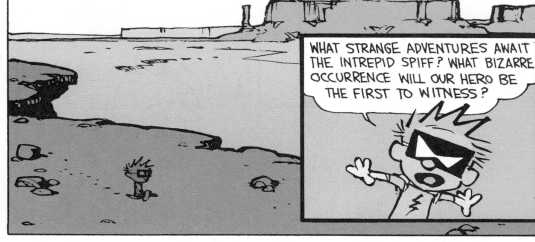

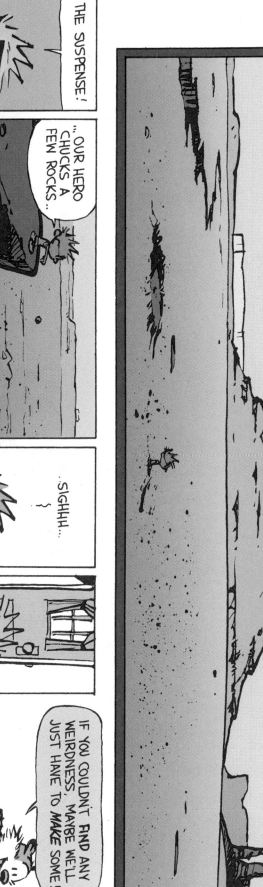

BOY, OUR FAMILY WOULD SURE BE IN TROUBLE IF ***YOU*** WERE BRINGING HOME THE BACON!
I AM NOT BACON!

OUCHYWAWA.
I'VE GOT A BIG OWWY BOO BOO ON MY PINKY.
THAT'S TOO BAD.

WHEN YOUR AILMENTS SOUND CUTE, YOU DON'T GET MUCH SYMPATHY.

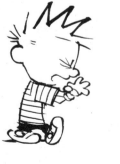

WHEN BIRDS BURP, IT MUST TASTE LIKE BUGS.

NOBODY EVER PAYS ME A PENNY FOR MY THOUGHTS.
WATTERSON

LOOK AT THIS, HOBBES. I ADDED IT UP AND FIGURED OUT I SPEND AN AVERAGE OF FOUR DAYS A YEAR TAKING BATHS!
FOUR FULL DAYS - MORNING, NOON, AND NIGHT - JUST SITTING IN THE STUPID BATHTUB! WHAT COULD POSSIBLY BE A BIGGER WASTE OF TIME THAN THAT ?!
HOW LONG DID IT TAKE YOU TO ADD THIS ALL UP?
WATTERSON

WOW, LOOK AT THIS BUG GO! WHAT ON EARTH WOULD MAKE A BUG HURRY?
YOU'RE DELUDING YOURSELF, STUPID! NOTHING YOU DO IS IMPORTANT! YOU'RE JUST A BUG!
OH MY GOSH, LOOK AT THE TIME!

I'M A MAN OF FEW WORDS.
MAYBE IF YOU READ MORE, YOU'D HAVE A LARGER VOCABULARY.

calvin and HOBBES by WATTERSON
BWA HA HA HA HA
EE HEE HEE HEE HEE
EHH HEH HEH HEH
..A LITTLE MORE... ..A LITTLE MORE...
PFOOSH!
AAA!
I WON'T FILL THIS ONE SO FULL.
THERE! PERFECT!
HEH- HEH
DARN KNOT! ACKK BLPP!
STOP IT! PBTT! IT'S TOO SLIPPERY! ACKPTH! BLP!
NOW LOOK, IT'S ALMOST EMPTY! I'LL HAVE TO FILL IT AGAIN.
STUPID BALLOON.
..A LITTLE MORE... AH! PERFECT!
IT SLIPPED OFF!
FWOOSH!
DOGGONE IT! HOBBES WILL BE HERE ANY SECOND AND...
YAAA
OH NO! AAAAA!
GEE, WHAT'S THE POINT?

IT'S HOT, IT'S HUMID, IT'S BUGGY, THERE'S NO BREEZE, AND THE AIR IS FULL OF POLLEN.
BUT IT'S **SUMMER**!

HEY ANT, YOU'RE WORKING LIKE A MANIAC AND WHAT HAVE YOU GOT TO SHOW FOR IT?
WHAT'S THE COLONY DONE FOR **YOU** LATELY? WHAT ABOUT **YOUR** NEEDS?
YOU DON'T OWE ANYBODY ANYTHING! LET THE OTHERS FEND FOR THEMSELVES! MOVE OUT! DISCOVER YOURSELF! EXPRESS YOUR INDIVIDUALITY!
IF THEY LISTEN, THIS SHOULD SOLVE OUR ANT PROBLEM.

HELLO?
IT SURRRRRE IS NICE OUTSIDE! CLIMB A TREE! GOOF OFF!
CLICK

DAD HARASSES ME WITH ***HIS*** VALUES, SO I HARASS HIM WITH MINE.

LOOK! I CAUGHT A BUTTERFLY!
IF PEOPLE COULD PUT RAINBOWS IN ZOOS, THEY'D DO IT.

AAAAAA

YOU'RE AWAKE? OH BOY! LET'S GO!
N-NO C-COFFEE F-FOR M-ME, TH-THANKS.
HEHH HOO HEHH
WATTERSON

WHY DOES ICE FLOAT?

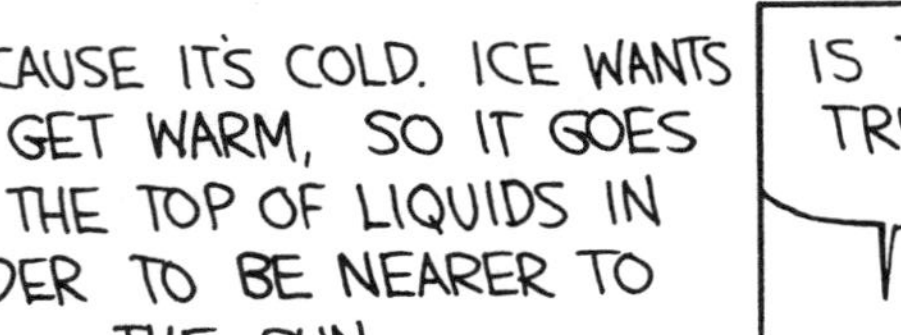
BECAUSE IT'S COLD. ICE WANTS TO GET WARM, SO IT GOES TO THE TOP OF LIQUIDS IN ORDER TO BE NEARER TO THE SUN.
IS THAT TRUE?
LOOK IT UP AND FIND OUT.

I SHOULD JUST LOOK STUFF UP IN THE FIRST PLACE.
YOU CAN LEARN A LOT, TALKING TO ME.
WATTERSON

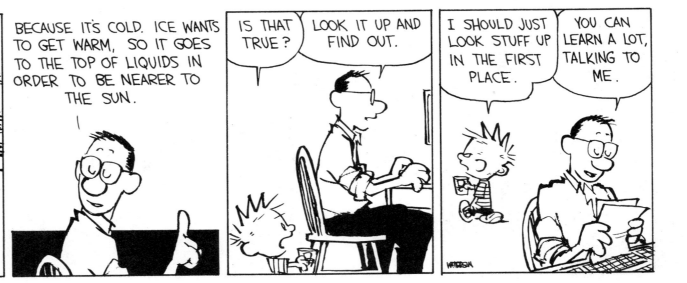

CALVIN AND HOBBES

BY WATTERSON

HOBBES GAVE ME THE STORY IDEA. FLIP THE PAGES AGAIN!

THIS WAS **MY** BOOK!

I CLEANED AND OILED YOUR BICYCLE, CALVIN. WHAT DO YOU SAY I TAKE SOME TIME AND HELP YOU LEARN HOW TO RIDE IT?
!

NO-O-O-O-O-O!!

YOU'RE WELCOME.
MOM! MOM! DAD **HATES** ME!
I'VE GOT THE BIKE, CALVIN. IT'S NOT GOING ANYWHERE.
I CAN FEEL IT'S GOING TO THROW ME! GET READY TO YANK ITS WHEELS OFF!

JUST RELAX. I'VE GOT YOU.
HOW CAN I RELAX?! I'M UNINSURED AND UNARMED! I'M AS GOOD AS DEAD!

PUSH BACK ON THE PEDALS. THAT'S YOUR BRAKE, OK?
YES, WELL, THAT WAS FUN! THANKS FOR THE LESSON!

GET BACK HERE.
NO, REALLY, I THINK I'VE GOT IT! YOU CAN SELL THE BIKE NOW.

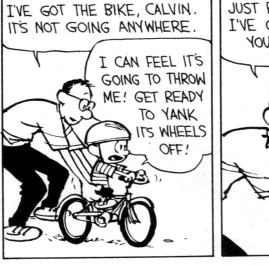

THE TRICK TO BALANCING IS TO HAVE A LITTLE FORWARD MOMENTUM.
AAA! NO MOMENTUM! NO MOMENTUM!

JUST PEDAL SLOWLY. I'M HOLDING THE BIKE, SO YOU WON'T FALL.
YOU'LL LET GO AND THE BIKE WILL LAUNCH ME INTO THE IONOSPHERE!

TRUST ME, OK?
TRUST YOU? I HARDLY KNOW YOU!

I'M YOUR FATHER!!
WHAT, FOR SIX YEARS?! WHEN I'M 40, WE'LL SEE HOW THINGS ARE GOING!

LOOK CALVIN, YOU'VE GOT TO RELAX A LITTLE. YOUR BALANCE WILL BE BETTER IF YOU'RE LOOSE.
I CAN'T HELP IT! IMMINENT DEATH MAKES ME TENSE! I ADMIT IT!

YOU NEED A GOAL. CONCENTRATE ON YOUR GOAL.
MY GOAL IS TO DISMANTLE THIS BICYCLE AND MAIL EVERY PIECE TO A DIFFERENT COUNTRY SO IT CAN NEVER BE REBUILT!

OK, THAT'S NOT A GOOD GOAL.
WELL I'M NOT CHANGING IT!

THINK ABOUT THE PLACES YOU CAN GO ONCE YOU LEARN HOW TO RIDE!
AAAA A

THINK ABOUT HOW IMPRESSED YOUR FRIENDS WILL BE! THINK ABOUT HOW MUCH FUN YOU'LL HAVE!
AAAA AAA

AAAA A AAAA AA

THINK ABOUT INHALING.
EEEP
AHHH..

OOH, IT DOESN'T LOOK LIKE THE BIKE LESSON WENT SO GOOD.
IT DIDN'T.

DAD **LIKES** RIDING HIS BIKE! HE DOESN'T UNDERSTAND WHAT IT'S LIKE FOR ME!

I **HATE** FLIPPING OVER THE BARS, GETTING CHASED AROUND THE YARD, AND GETTING MOWED DOWN BY A DEMONIC MACHINE!

IS THAT WHAT HAPPENED?
NO, I TRIPPED COMING UP THE STAIRS.

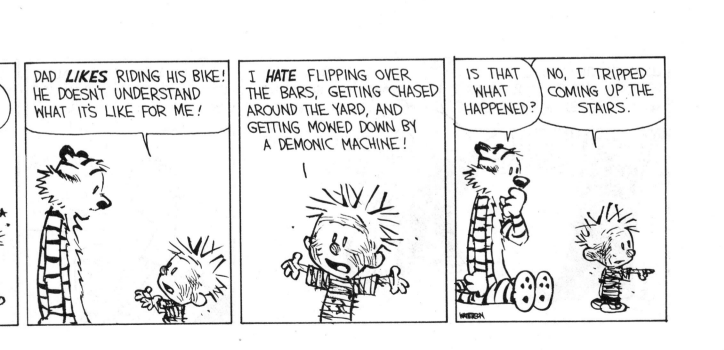

DING DONG
I'M COMING, I'M COMING.
AAAA!
RRR!
I OPENED THE DOOR AND MY BIKE GOT IN!!
HELLPP!
RUN FOR YOUR LIVES!! IT'S AN UNBALANCED BICYCLE!!
calvin and HobbES by WATTERSON
SOMEBODY GET ME A SPOKE WRENCH!
HEHH HOO HEHH HOO
BACK! BACK!
SLAM
HA! YOU CAN'T GET ME NOW!
AIEE! TIRE TRACKS ON THE RUGS! OIL ON THE COUCH!
WHERE'S THAT KID?!
SOMEDAY THE NEIGHBORS WILL LOOK OUT AND WONDER WHY THERE'S A GROWN MAN WEARING KIDS' CLOTHES ON OUR ROOF.

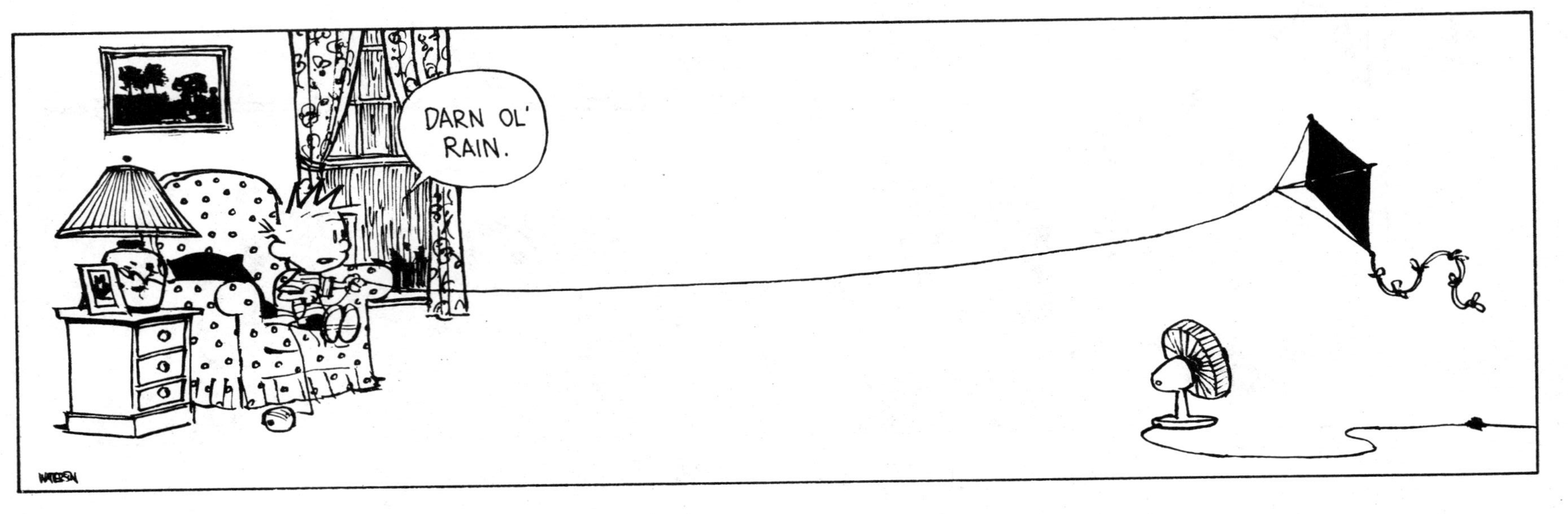
DARN OL' RAIN.
WATTERSON

IT'S NOT SUMMER IF YOUR TONGUE ISN'T PURPLE.
WATTERSON

WHAT DOES IT MEAN WHEN SOMEONE SAYS TO "GIVE IT THE OL' COLLEGE TRY"?
IT MEANS YOU JOIN YOUR FRIENDS, GET SOME CHEAP BEER, ORDER A PIZZA, AND FORGET ABOUT TOMORROW.
THAT'S NOT WHAT IT MEANS!
WHERE DID ***YOU*** GO TO COLLEGE?
NEVER MIND.

CAAAAAA
ALLLLLLY
VINNNNNN,
THAAAAA
T'S EEEN
OUUGHHH.
M-MOM S-SURE WAS M-MOVINGG ST-STRANGELLLY T-TODDAYY.
MAYBE SHE'S RIGHT ABOUT HOW MUCH SUGAR YOU PUT ON THAT CEREAL.

FRANK appraisal OF YOUR LOOKS 50¢
ANY BUSINESS?
NOT SO FAR.
FRANK appraisal OF YOUR LOOKS 50¢
BUT I'M GIVING OUT LOTS OF FREE SAMPLES.
FRANK

WHAT A LOVELY DAY FOR A HIKE!
IT'S NOT SO BAD **THIS** WAY!
NO, WE WON'T CARRY YOU. STOP GRIPING.
THIS IS SO MUCH WORK!

Calvin and Hobbes by Watterson
WELCOME TO STUPIDOPOLIS...
..A THRIVING COASTAL CITY...
..STUPIDLY BUILT NEAR AN UNDERSEA FAULT LINE...
..THAT JUST SHIFTED!
A CURIOUS SHADOW FALLS OVER DOWNTOWN.
RUMMBBBLLE
PLOOSHH
WHY DOES HE BUILD EVERYTHING SO CLOSE TO THE WATER? IT'S STUPID.
HE DOESN'T SEEM TO MIND DOING IT OVER AND OVER.

LOOK AT THIS! MOM GOT ME A BOOK FROM THE LIBRARY.
THAT'S NICE.

NICE?!? IT'S ***SUMMER***! I ONLY GET THREE SHORT MONTHS TO GOOF OFF! I'M NOT GOING TO WASTE THESE PRECIOUS DAYS READING ***BOOKS***!
SUMMERS ARE FOR VEGETATING! THAT'S WHY THE TV SHOWS ARE RERUNS AND THE MOVIES ARE SEQUELS!
NO WONDER THE FLIES COME OUT.
HECK, EVERYONE ***KNOWS*** IT'S NOT ENTERTAINMENT UNLESS YOU CAN SIT IN THE DARK AND EAT.

HEY, ARE YOU READING THAT BOOK MOM GOT ME FROM THE LIBRARY?
MM-HMM.

IS IT GOOD? DO YOU LIKE IT? IS IT EXCITING? ARE YOU HAVING FUN?
SHH.
HOW COULD IT POSSIBLY BE FUN WHEN IT'S SO ***QUIET***?!?

I READ THIS LIBRARY BOOK YOU GOT ME.

WHAT DID YOU THINK OF IT?

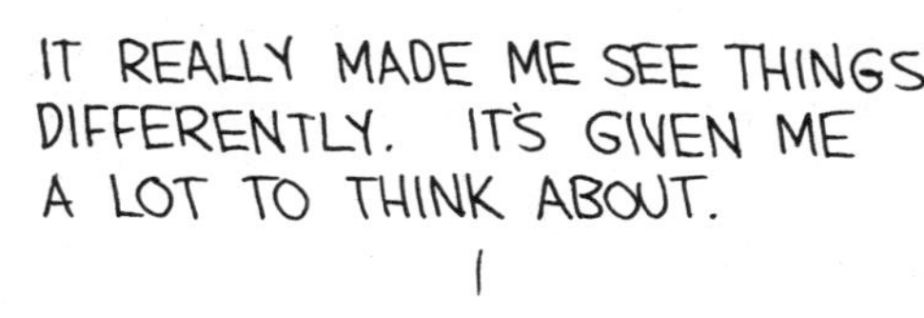

I'M WRITING A FUND-RAISING LETTER.
THE SECRET TO GETTING DONATIONS IS TO DEPICT EVERYONE WHO DISAGREES WITH YOU AS THE ENEMY. THEN YOU EXPLAIN HOW THEY'RE SYSTEMATICALLY WORKING TO DESTROY EVERYTHING YOU HOLD DEAR.
IT'S A WAR OF VALUES! RATIONAL DISCUSSION IS HOPELESS! COMPROMISE IS UNTHINKABLE! OUR ONLY HOPE IS WELL-FUNDED ANTAGONISM, SO WE NEED YOUR MONEY TO KEEP UP THE FIGHT!

HOW CYNICALLY UNCONSTRUCTIVE.
ENMITY SELLS.
WATTERSON

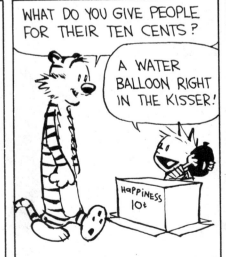

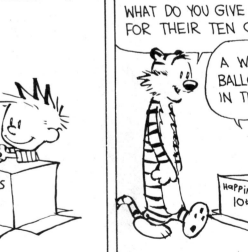

HAPPINESS 10¢
WHAT DO YOU GIVE PEOPLE FOR THEIR TEN CENTS?
A WATER BALLOON RIGHT IN THE KISSER!
HAPPINESS 10¢

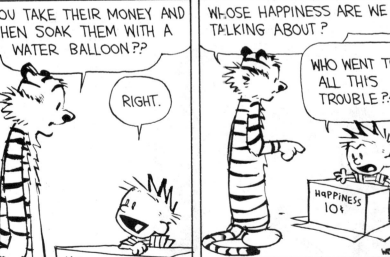

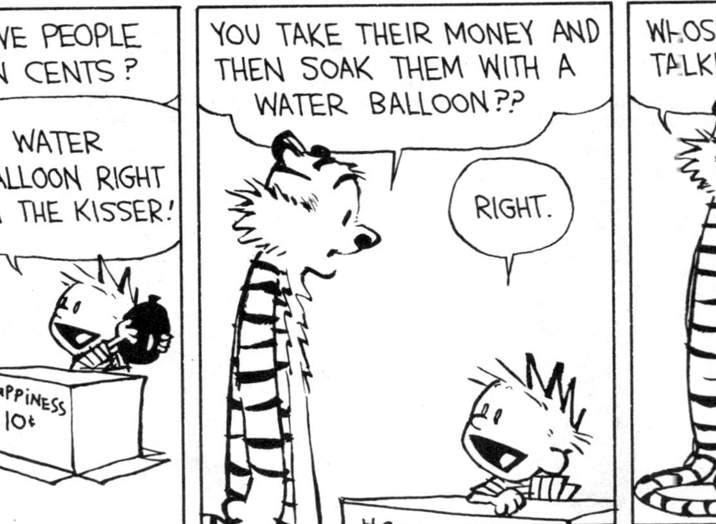
YOU TAKE THEIR MONEY AND THEN SOAK THEM WITH A WATER BALLOON??
RIGHT.
WHOSE HAPPINESS ARE WE TALKING ABOUT?
WHO WENT TO ALL THIS TROUBLE?!
HAPPINESS 10¢
WATTERSON

calvin and HOBBES
I ORDERED THE TWO TONS OF TENDERLOIN.
OH YES. DRIVE AROUND TO THE LOADING DOCK AND I'LL GET THE FORKLIFT.
CALVIN, LUNCHTIME!
by WATTERSON
MAYONNAISE?! I LIKE MUSTARD!
MAYBE YOU SHOULD FIX YOUR OWN TRICERATOPS SANDWICH.

HOW TALL
ARE YOU?

OK, THE MAP SAYS TO TURN LEFT AT THIS TREE AND WALK 30 PACES.
..29...30. WHAT'S HERE?
MY MAP SHOWS A BIG HOLE.
WOULDN'T IT BE FASTER TO MAKE THE **MAP** CONFORM TO THE **YARD**?
ARE YOU IN SOME SORT OF HURRY?

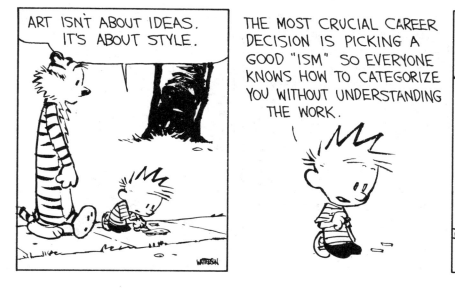

YOU THINK YOU'RE SO DARN SMART!

ART ISN'T ABOUT IDEAS. IT'S ABOUT STYLE.
THE MOST CRUCIAL CAREER DECISION IS PICKING A GOOD "ISM" SO EVERYONE KNOWS HOW TO CATEGORIZE YOU WITHOUT UNDERSTANDING THE WORK.

YOU DO GOOFY DRAWINGS ON THE SIDEWALK.
RIGHT. I'M A SUBURBAN POST-MODERNIST.

AREN'T WE ALL.
I WAS GOING TO BE A NEO-DECONSTRUCTIVIST BUT MOM WOULDN'T LET ME.

COULDN'T YOU SUPPORT YOUR ART WITH ANOTHER JOB?

WHAT, YOU MEAN **WORK**?

BUT REALLY, ART IS A PRIVATE LANGUAGE FOR SOPHISTICATES TO CONGRATULATE THEMSELVES ON THEIR SUPERIORITY TO THE REST OF THE WORLD.

YOU MISSPELLED "WELTANSCHAUUNG."

A GOOD ARTIST'S STATEMENT SAYS MORE THAN HIS ART EVER DOES.

Calvin and Hobbes
by WATTERSON
LOOK, A SNAKE!
A BIG ONE!
DO YOU THINK IT'S POISONOUS?
BEATS ME. HOW CAN YOU TELL?
IF IT BITES YOU AND YOU DIE, IT'S POISONOUS.
HAR HAR.
LOOK HOW IT GLIDES ALONG. IT'S ALMOST LIKE A LIQUID.
I WONDER HOW THEY DO THAT.
HE'S FLICKING HIS TONGUE OUT.
I THINK THAT'S HOW THEY SMELL, BUT WHY WOULD THEY SMELL WITH A TONGUE?
DO SNAKES HAVE EYELIDS? DO THEY SLEEP WITH THEIR EYES OPEN?
DON'T SNAKES EAT MICE? HOW COULD A SNAKE SWALLOW SOMETHING BIGGER THAN ITS OWN HEAD?
HECK, WE DON'T KNOW **ANYTHING** ABOUT SNAKES.
MAYBE YOUR MOM WOULD GET US A BOOK.
YEAH, LET'S GO SEE!
WE'LL BE EXPERTS! WE'LL LEARN ALL THERE IS TO KNOW!
HEY, WAIT A MINUTE! IT'S SUMMER! I'M ON VACATION! I DON'T WANT TO **LEARN** ANYTHING!
IF NOBODY MAKES YOU DO IT, IT COUNTS AS FUN.
HMM... YOU REALLY THINK SO?!
COOOOOOLLL.

NOTHING IS PERMANENT. EVERYTHING CHANGES. THAT'S THE ONE THING WE KNOW FOR SURE IN THIS WORLD.
BUT I'M STILL GOING TO GRIPE ABOUT IT.

PLOOSH
HOW CAN SOMETHING SEEM SO PLAUSIBLE AT THE TIME AND SO IDIOTIC IN RETROSPECT?

I REFUSE TO TAKE OUT THE GARBAGE! I HAVE THE RIGHT TO DO WHATEVER I WANT, ALL THE TIME!

NO YOU DON'T.
I DON'T?

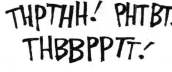

WELL IT SURE **OUGHT** TO BE A RIGHT.

BU-UURRPPP

THPTHH! PHTBT! THBBPPTT!

BU-UURRRPP

WHAT ARE YOU DOING?
I'M HOPING THERE'S A MOCKINGBIRD AROUND.

HELLO? NO, MY DAD'S NOT HERE RIGHT NOW.

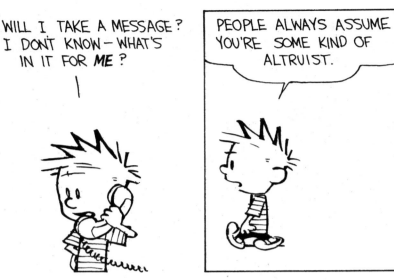

WILL I TAKE A MESSAGE? I DON'T KNOW – WHAT'S IN IT FOR **ME**?

PEOPLE ALWAYS ASSUME YOU'RE SOME KIND OF ALTRUIST.

OH, JUST SO YOU KNOW...

I AM THE DOWNHILL TUMBLE AND ROLL CHAMP, KING OF THE TOAD FINDERS, CAPTAIN OF THE HIGH ALTITUDE TREE BRANCH VISTA CLUB, SECOND PLACE FINISHER IN THE 'ROUND THE YARD BACKWARD DASH, PREMIER BURPER STATE DIVISION, SODBUSTER AND WORM SCOUT FIRST ORDER, AND GENERALISSIMO OF THE MUD AND MAYHEM SOCIETY!

BUSY DAY?
ABOUT USUAL. WANT TO HEAR WHAT HOBBES IS?

Calvin and Hobbes by WATTERSON

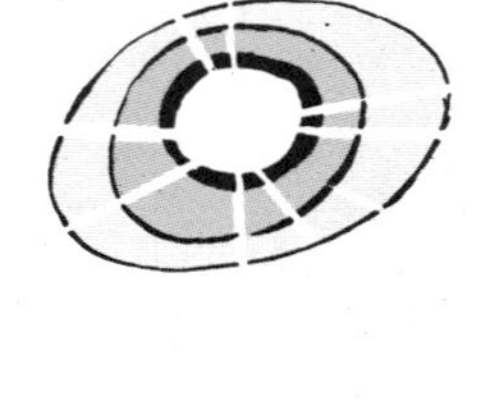

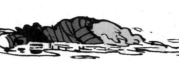

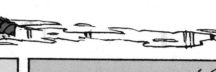

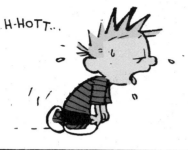

PEOPLE ASK WHY WE TOLERATE A POPULAR CULTURE THAT CELEBRATES VIOLENCE AND DEPRAVITY.
BECAUSE IT'S ENTERTAINING, THAT'S WHY!
IF WARPED VALUES ARE THE PRICE OF A VICARIOUS THRILL, SO BE IT! LET THE BUSINESS RESPOND TO CONSUMER DEMAND!
THE CUSTOMER IS ALWAYS RIGHT.
SHOCK AND TITILLATE ME! I'VE GOT MONEY!

POPULAR CULTURE ISN'T TO BLAME FOR SELLING TWISTED VALUES.
MOVIES, RECORDS, AND TV SHOWS REFLECT THE REALITY OF OUR TIMES. ARTISTS DEPICT HATRED AND VIOLENCE BECAUSE THAT'S WHAT THEY SEE.
WHY DON'T THEY SEE THINGS OF BEAUTY AND VALUE?
BECAUSE BORING STUFF DOESN'T SELL.
SUCH VISION AND INTEGRITY.
THERE'S NOTHING LIKE A GOOD GUNFIGHT TO UPLIFT THE SPIRIT.

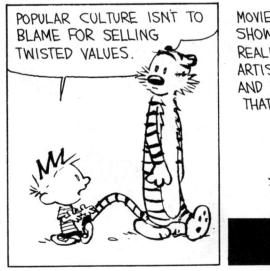

ANOTHER THING TO REMEMBER ABOUT POPULAR CULTURE IS THAT TODAY'S TV-REARED AUDIENCE IS HIP AND SOPHISTICATED. THIS STUFF DOESN'T AFFECT US.

WE CAN SEPARATE FACT FROM FICTION. WE UNDERSTAND SATIRE AND IRONY. WE'RE DETACHED AND JADED VIEWERS WHO AREN'T INFLUENCED BY WHAT WE WATCH.

I THINK I HEAR ADVERTISERS LAUGHING.
HOLD ON, I NEED TO INFLATE MY BASKETBALL SHOES.
WATTERSON

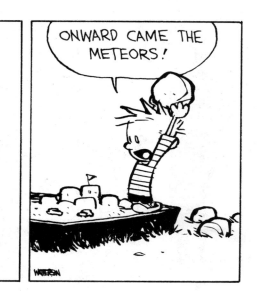

ONWARD CAME THE METEORS!
WATTERSON

BUGS GET ON MY NERVES!
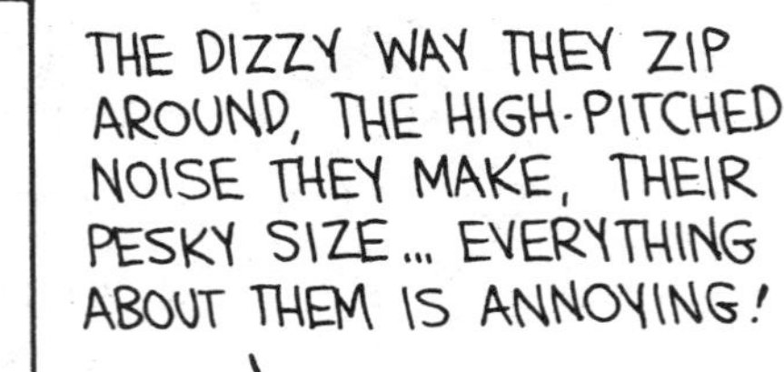
THE DIZZY WAY THEY ZIP AROUND, THE HIGH-PITCHED NOISE THEY MAKE, THEIR PESKY SIZE... EVERYTHING ABOUT THEM IS ANNOYING!

...SAID THE HYPERACTIVE, WHINY, SMALL CHILD.
!

I WANT YOU TO PICK UP YOUR ROOM TODAY, OK?
DO I GET PAID?

NO.

IF I DON'T GET PAID, HOW DO I KNOW IT'S IMPORTANT?!

YOU CAN TRUST A MOTHER ON THAT.

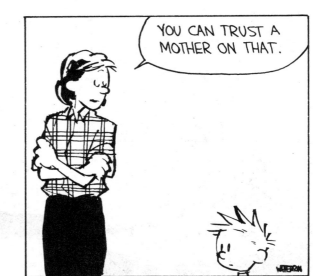

WE ALL WANT MEANINGFUL LIVES. WE LOOK FOR MEANING IN EVERYTHING WE DO.
BUT SUPPOSE THERE *IS* NO MEANING! SUPPOSE LIFE IS FUNDAMENTALLY ABSURD!
calvin and HoBBES
by WATTERSON
SUPPOSE THERE'S NO REASON, OR TRUTH, OR RIGHTNESS IN ANYTHING!
WHAT IF NOTHING MEANS ANYTHING? WHAT IF NOTHING REALLY MATTERS?
I GUESS THERE'S NO HARM IN A LITTLE WISHFUL THINKING.
OR SUPPOSE *EVERYTHING* MATTERS. WHICH WOULD BE WORSE?!

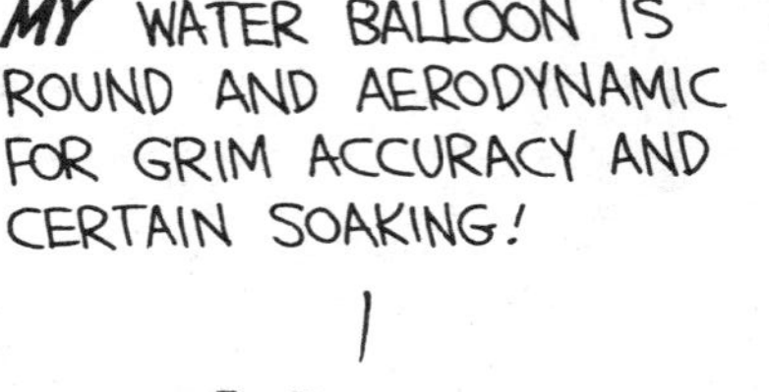
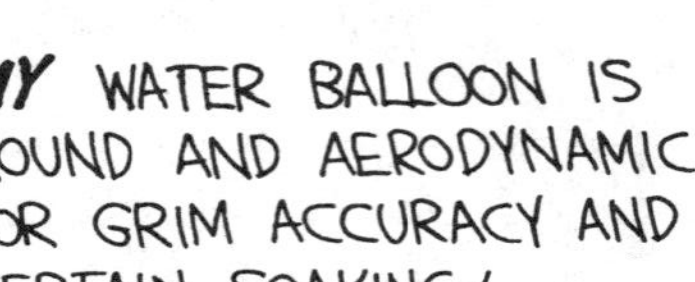
MY WATER BALLOON IS ROUND AND AERODYNAMIC FOR GRIM ACCURACY AND CERTAIN SOAKING!

YOUR WATER BALLOON IS LONG AND FLOPPY, IMPOSSIBLE TO THROW THE SLIGHTEST DISTANCE!

THE ADVANTAGE IS CLEARLY MINE! DO YOU SURRENDER?

WATTERSON

HEY, THERE'S NO BUTTER IN THE BUTTER DISH! MY TOAST WILL GET COLD WHILE I GET ANOTHER STICK FROM THE FRIDGE!
BUT

HAVEN'T I SUFFERED ENOUGH?!? WHERE WILL IT ALL END?!?
BUT

MR. AND MRS. EMPATHY.
WATTERSON

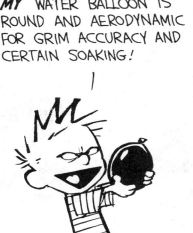

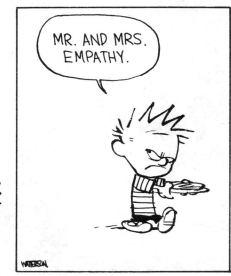

I'M GLAD YOU'RE GETTING SOME EXERCISE. KEEP THAT HEART RATE UP.

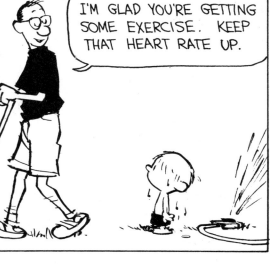

DAD CAN TAKE THE FUN OUT OF **ANY**THING.
WATTERSON

I HAVE A HAMMER!

I CAN PUT THINGS TOGETHER! I CAN KNOCK THINGS APART! I CAN ALTER MY ENVIRONMENT AT WILL AND MAKE AN INCREDIBLE DIN ALL THE WHILE!

AH, IT'S GREAT TO BE MALE!
WATTERSON

VAMPIRE BUGS! RUN FOR YOUR LIFE!
THEY'RE CALLED MOSQUITOS.

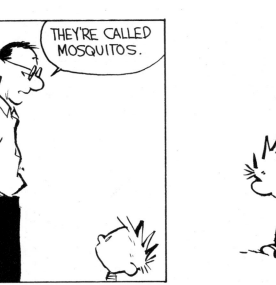

SO IF THEY DRINK YOUR BLOOD, YOU DON'T TURN INTO ONE?
WATTERSON

WHEN A PERSON PAUSES IN MID-SENTENCE TO CHOOSE A WORD, THAT'S THE BEST TIME TO JUMP IN AND CHANGE THE SUBJECT!

IT'S LIKE AN INTERCEPTION IN FOOTBALL! YOU GRAB THE OTHER GUY'S IDEA AND RUN THE OPPOSITE WAY WITH IT!

THE MORE SENTENCES YOU COMPLETE, THE HIGHER YOUR SCORE! THE IDEA IS TO BLOCK THE OTHER GUY'S THOUGHTS AND EXPRESS YOUR OWN! THAT'S HOW YOU WIN!

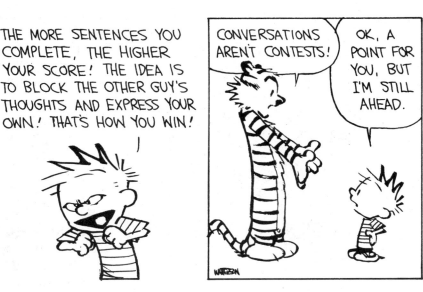

CONVERSATIONS AREN'T CONTESTS!
OK, A POINT FOR YOU, BUT I'M STILL AHEAD.
WATTERSON

Calvin and Hobbes by WATTERSON

OH BOY! IT'S BEDTIME!

SPROINGG

WOOOOOO

WULP!

FWAPP

SHOONK

SHOOOSHHH

SPLOOSH

WAA!!

SHOOP

FLIP

THWUPP

OOF!

..AHHH...

BEDTIME. LET'S GO.

AWW, I HATE GETTING READY FOR BED.

JUST ONCE I'D LIKE TO SEE YOU MANAGE THIS DURING THE SCHOOL YEAR.
YAAAAAAA

ALMOST EVERYWHERE YOU GO, YOU CAN HEAR PEOPLE, RADIOS, AND ALL KINDS OF ENGINES.
WHEN YOU'RE ACTUALLY CONFRONTED WITH THE STILLNESS OF NATURE, IT'S KIND OF STARTLING.

WHY, YOU CAN EVEN HEAR YOURSELF THINK.
THIS IS MAKING ME NERVOUS. LET'S GO IN.

WE RELY ON SIGHT TO CONFIRM THE EXISTENCE OF THINGS. WE DON'T BELIEVE IN THINGS WE CAN'T SEE.

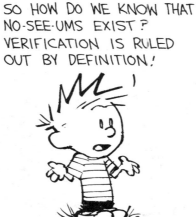

SO HOW DO WE KNOW THAT NO-SEE-UMS EXIST? VERIFICATION IS RULED OUT BY DEFINITION!

IT'S AN ONTOLOGICAL QUANDARY.
HOLD STILL A MOMENT.

OOH, I ITCH!
GLAD I COULD HELP.

CALVIN, TIME TO COME IN!

AWW MOM, IT'S NOT EVEN DARK YET!

I DIDN'T SAY IT WAS. I SAID IT'S TIME TO COME IN.

IT'S A CRUEL SEASON THAT MAKES YOU GET READY FOR BED WHILE IT'S LIGHT OUT.

SOME PEOPLE ARE PRAGMATISTS, TAKING THINGS AS THEY COME AND MAKING THE BEST OF THE CHOICES AVAILABLE.
SOME PEOPLE ARE IDEALISTS, STANDING FOR PRINCIPLE AND REFUSING TO COMPROMISE.
AND SOME PEOPLE JUST ACT ON ANY WHIM THAT ENTERS THEIR HEADS.
I WONDER WHICH *YOU* ARE.
I PRAGMATICALLY TURN MY WHIMS INTO PRINCIPLES!

TO HELP MOM PREPARE BETTER MEALS, I'M COMPILING A BOOK OF RECIPES.
I NOTICE THAT ALL OF THEM INVOLVE DEEP-FAT FRYING.
I'M ADDING A CHOCOLATE SYRUP SECTION NOW.

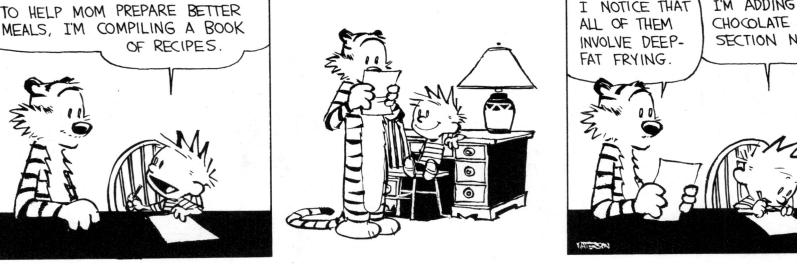

Calvin and Hobbes
by WATTERSON

HUP-
-PTCHOO
AAA!
THPKXX!
HAYFEVER SEASON ISN'T ALL BAD.
YOU THIG ID'S FUDDY, BUD ID'S DOT.
SLAM
THXXXPTB.!

IT'S HARD TO CONCEAL A WATER BALLOON.

I'VE GOT A WATER BALLOON HIDDEN UNDER THIS TURBAN! PRETTY INGENIOUS, HUH?
I'LL BET THE TOWEL COMES IN HANDY.
WHY?

COULDN'T I BE SEDATED FOR THIS?!
OH, DON'T I WISH.
IT USED TO BE THAT IF A CLIENT WANTED SOMETHING DONE IN A WEEK, IT WAS CONSIDERED A RUSH JOB, AND HE'D BE LUCKY TO GET IT.
NOW, WITH MODEMS, FAXES, AND CAR PHONES, EVERYBODY WANTS EVERYTHING INSTANTLY! IMPROVED TECHNOLOGY JUST INCREASES EXPECTATIONS.
THESE MACHINES DON'T MAKE LIFE EASIER – THEY MAKE LIFE MORE HARASSED.
SIX MINUTES TO MICROWAVE THIS?? WHO'S GOT THAT KIND OF TIME?!
IF WE WANTED MORE LEISURE, WE'D INVENT MACHINES THAT DO THINGS ***LESS*** EFFICIENTLY.

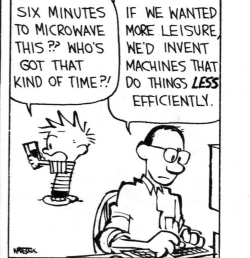

SUMMER IS BUTTER ON YOUR CHIN AND CORN MUSH BETWEEN EVERY TOOTH.
IT WAS NICE OF YOUR PARENTS TO LET US EAT OUTSIDE.

..EWWW..
AH! AH!
CHOOO!
THIS FOOD IS ALLERGIC TO ME.

Calvin and Hobbes by Watterson

MY MOM AND MY DAD ARE NOT WHAT THEY SEEM.
THEIR DULL APPEARANCE IS PART OF THEIR SCHEME.
I KNOW OF THEIR PLANS. I KNOW THEIR TECHNIQUES.
MY PARENTS ARE OUTER SPACE ALIEN FREAKS!

THEY LANDED ON EARTH IN SPACESHIPS HUMONGOUS.
POSING AS GROWNUPS, THEY NOW WALK AMONG US.
MY PARENTS DENY THIS, BUT I KNOW THE TRUTH.
THEY'RE HERE TO ENSLAVE ME AND SPOIL MY YOUTH.

EARLY EACH MORNING, AS THE SUN RISES,
MOM AND DAD PUT ON THEIR EARTHLING DISGUISES.
I KNEW RIGHT AWAY THEIR MASKS WEREN'T LEGIT.
THEIR FACES ARE LINED – THEY SAG AND DON'T FIT.

THE EARTH'S GRAVITY MAKES THEM SLUGGISH AND SLOW.
THEY SAY NOT TO RUN, WHEREVER I GO.
THEY LIVE BY THE CLOCK. THEY'RE SLAVES TO ROUTINES.
THEY WORK THE YEAR 'ROUND. THEY'RE ALMOST MACHINES.

THEY DENY THAT TV AND FRIED FOOD HAVE MUCH WORTH.
THEY CANNOT BE HUMAN. THEY'RE NOT OF THIS EARTH.
I CANNOT ESCAPE THEIR ALIEN GAZE,
AND THEY'RE WARPING MY MIND WITH THEIR ALIEN WAYS.
FOR SINISTER PLOTS, THIS ONE IS A GEM.
THEY'RE BRINGING ME UP TO TURN *ME* INTO *THEM!*

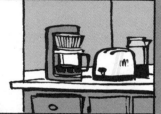

I'M A FIREFLY.
I SEE THE FLASHLIGHT.

DO WE HAVE ANY STRING?
SURE. WHAT FOR?
A WICK. I'M SAVING ALL MY EAR WAX TO MAKE A CANDLE.
OH CALVIN! BLAUGHH!
COULD I MAKE A SET OF CRAYONS?

I'M FILLING OUT A READER SURVEY FOR *CHEWING* MAGAZINE.

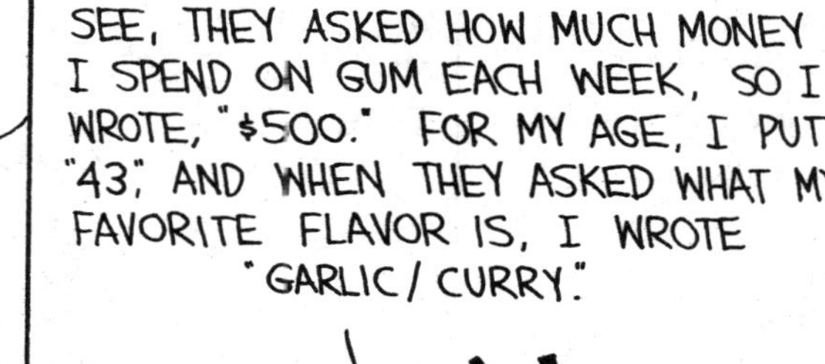

SEE, THEY ASKED HOW MUCH MONEY I SPEND ON GUM EACH WEEK, SO I WROTE, "$500." FOR MY AGE, I PUT "43," AND WHEN THEY ASKED WHAT MY FAVORITE FLAVOR IS, I WROTE "GARLIC / CURRY."
CHEWING

THIS MAGAZINE SHOULD HAVE SOME AMUSING ADS SOON.
I LOVE MESSING WITH DATA.

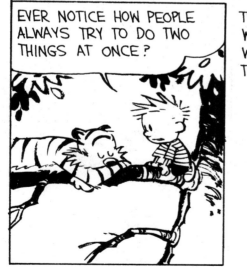

EVER NOTICE HOW PEOPLE ALWAYS TRY TO DO TWO THINGS AT ONCE?
THEY TALK ON THE PHONE WHILE THEY DRIVE, THEY WATCH TV WHILE THEY EAT, THEY LISTEN TO MUSIC WHILE THEY WORK...

PEOPLE NEVER FOCUS ON ANY ONE THING TO ENJOY IT OR DO IT WELL.

YOU'RE BREAKING MY CONCENTRATION.
WE FOCUS ON DOING NOTHING AT ALL!

I CAN'T BELIEVE SUMMER IS ALMOST OVER.
SOON SCHOOL WILL START. NO MORE FREEDOM, NO MORE LONG DAYS OUTSIDE, NO MORE FUN.
WELL, LET'S GO MAKE THE MOST OF THE TIME WE HAVE LEFT!
NAH, I'VE RESERVED THE REST OF THE MONTH FOR MOPING.

HEH HEH! IF I MISS MY TARGET, **THIS** WATER BALLOON IS REUSABLE!

BAD IDEA.

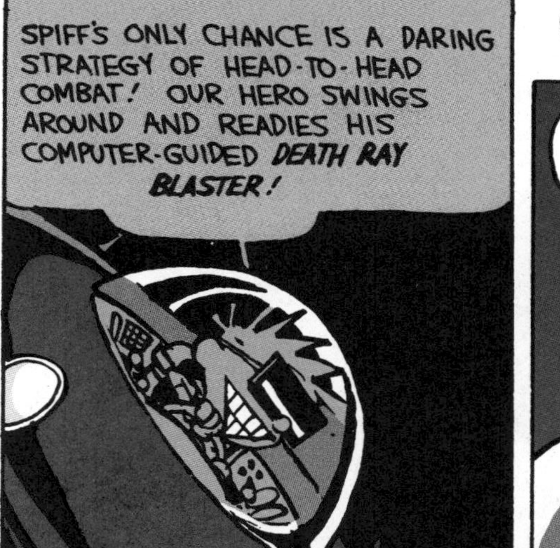

Calvin and Hobbes by WATTERSON

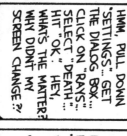

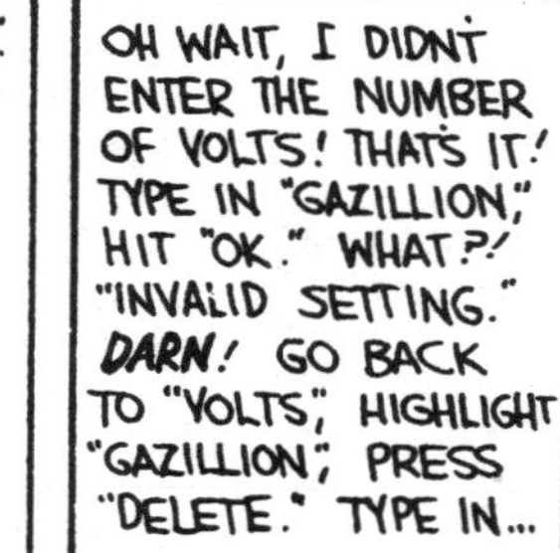

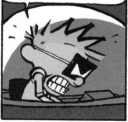

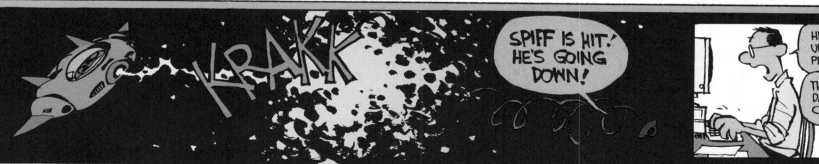

LOOK! A QUARTER!!

WOW! I'M RICH BEYOND MY DREAMS! I CAN HAVE ANYTHING I WANT! ALL MY PRAYERS HAVE BEEN ANSWERED!

MAYBE THERE'S MORE.

I'D BUILD A RAFT FOR THIS POND, BUT I DON'T HAVE A PLACE TO DOCK IT.
I'VE ALWAYS SAID YOU'RE A FRIEND WITHOUT PIER.
HUH?

NOTHING.
MM.
I GUESS YOU'RE UNDER A LOT OF PIER PRESSURE.
IS SOMETHING WRONG WITH YOU?!

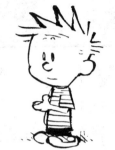

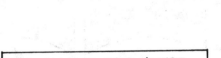

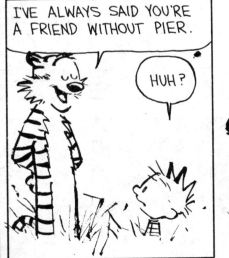

HERE'S STINKY, THE TALKING SOCK! HI, STINKY! SAY SOMETHING TO SUSIE!

HELLO, YOU UGLY BUCKET OF BOOGERS!

THAT DARN "THROW YOUR VOICE" AD MADE IT SOUND LIKE EVERYONE WOULD BE FOOLED.
!

THERE AREN'T MANY HEROES THESE DAYS.

WHO IS OUT THERE TO INSPIRE US WITH A PERSONAL EXAMPLE OF VIRTUE AND SELF-SACRIFICE IN THE NAME OF A HIGHER GOOD?

WHO CAN WE LOOK UP TO? BUSINESS LEADERS? SPORTS FIGURES? POLITICIANS? CELEBRITIES? HECK, WE'RE LUCKY IF THEY DON'T END UP IN PRISON!

FORTUNATELY, IF WE CAN'T GET INSPIRATION, WE'LL ACCEPT ENTERTAINMENT.
AS USUAL, THE HERO BUSINESS IS UP TO ME.

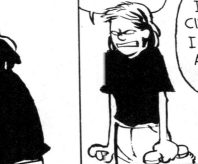

HELLO? MM-HMM... NO THANK YOU, I'M NOT INTERESTED.

HMM? ... NO, I DON'T WANT... MM... AS I SAID, I DON'T... MM-HMM.. NO, I ... MM.. LOOK, I'M NOT... HMM?..
DID IT EVER OCCUR TO YOU THAT I HAVE A LIFE BEYOND THIS SALES PITCH AND YOU'RE INTRUDING ON IT?!

THERE WOULD BE MORE CIVILITY IN THIS WORLD IF PEOPLE DIDN'T TAKE IT AS AN INVITATION TO WALK ON YOU.
I'M ONLY CIVIL BECAUSE I DON'T KNOW ANY SWEAR WORDS.

HOLD IT. WAIT, I NEED TO...

KACHOOO!

WOW, THIS IS YOUR BEST DRIVER'S LICENSE PHOTO **EVER**!
UNTIL THIS EXPIRES, I WILL BE DRIVING **EXACTLY** THE SPEED LIMIT!

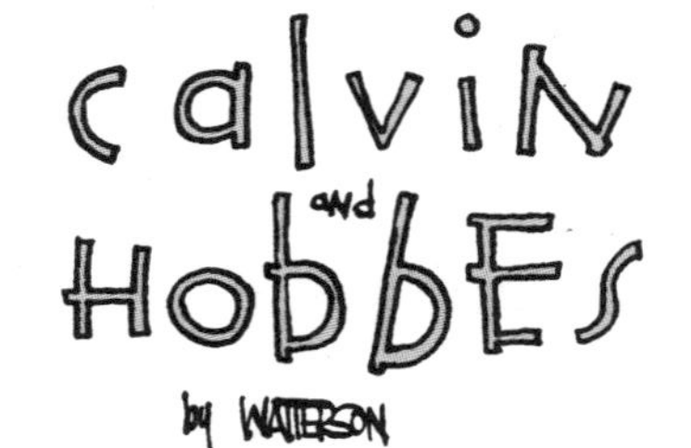
calvin and Hobbes
by WATTERSON

DID YOU KNOW THAT NOBODY ON OUR STREET SETS AN ALARM CLOCK IN THE MORNING?
SHUT UP.

HOBBES IS ALLOWED TO EAT AT THE TABLE WITH ME TONIGHT?
AND WE GET TO EAT EARLY AND HAVE GRILLED CHEESE SANDWICHES? THIS IS MORE LIKE IT!
BOY, YOU LOOK NICE.
THANK YOU.
...UH-OH.
DIBS ON THE FRENCH FRIES.

CALVIN, IF YOU RUN THESE STOCKINGS...! DEAR, GRAB HIM!
NO! NO! NOT ROSALYN! AAAAAAAAAAA! HELP! DON'T LEAVE ME!!
..AND THE NEIGHBORS' NUMBERS ARE (PULL A LEG, WILL YOU?) BY THE PHONE.
I TOLD YOU MY RATES DOUBLED, RIGHT?

OK CALVIN, LISTEN UP.
AAA! NO! I'M NOT GOING TO BED! YOU CAN'T MAKE ME!
YOU AND I ARE GOING TO MAKE A DEAL.
A DEAL?! WHAT KIND OF DEAL?? I'M NOT MAKING ANY DEAL!
YOU DON'T GIVE ME ANY TROUBLE TONIGHT, AND WE'LL PLAY A GAME.
WHAT'S THE GAME? "KILL THE KID"?! NO WAY!
PLUS, YOU GET TO STAY UP HALF AN HOUR PAST YOUR BEDTIME.
NOTICE HOW OBEDIENTLY I'M SITTING HERE.
WATTERSON

SO WHAT'S THE GAME I GET TO PLAY IF I'M GOOD?
YOU CAN DECIDE. PICK YOUR FAVORITE GAME.
IS THIS A TRICK? CAN WE REALLY PLAY MY FAVORITE GAME??
SURE, WHY NOT? WHAT IS IT?
CALVINBALL!!
CALVIN-BALL??
GET OUT THE TIME-FRACTURE WICKETS, HOBBES! WE'RE GONNA PLAY CALVINBALL!
WHAT THE HECK IS CALVINBALL?
WATTERSON

AND IF I DO ALL MY HOMEWORK, WE GET TO STAY UP AN EXTRA HALF HOUR TO PLAY CALVINBALL!
OH BOY!
HERE, YOU CAN DOUBLE-CHECK MY MATH PROBLEMS WHILE I START ON MY HISTORY. WE'VE GOT TO GET THIS DONE.
YOU FINISHED YOUR MATH ??
WE'RE HERE TO HAVE A NICE TIME. TRY NOT TO THINK ABOUT ALL THE TROUBLE CALVIN'S GETTING INTO.
DID YOU HEAR THAT ?? IT SOUNDED LIKE ANOTHER SIREN.

I FINISHED ALL MY HOME-WORK, JUST LIKE YOU SAID TO, ROSALYN.
GREAT. ARE YOU READY TO PLAY YOUR GAME THEN?
FIRST WE NEED TO MAKE YOU A MASK.
A MASK? WHAT FOR?
WHEN YOU PLAY CALVINBALL, YOU WEAR A MASK.
WHY?
SORRY, NO ONE'S ALLOWED TO QUESTION THE MASKS.
THIS SOUNDS LIKE A GREAT GAME.

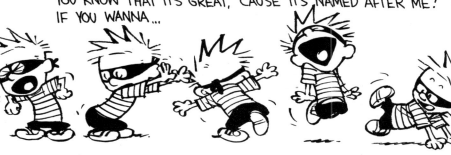

OTHER KIDS' GAMES ARE ALL SUCH A BORE!
THEY'VE GOTTA HAVE RULES AND THEY GOTTA KEEP SCORE!
CALVINBALL IS BETTER BY FAR!
IT'S NEVER THE SAME! IT'S ALWAYS BIZARRE!
YOU DON'T NEED A TEAM OR A REFEREE!
YOU KNOW THAT IT'S GREAT, 'CAUSE IT'S NAMED AFTER ME!
IF YOU WANNA...

UH, FEEL FREE TO HARMONIZE WITH HOBBES ON THE RUMMA TUM TUMS.
THIS WAS A MISTAKE.

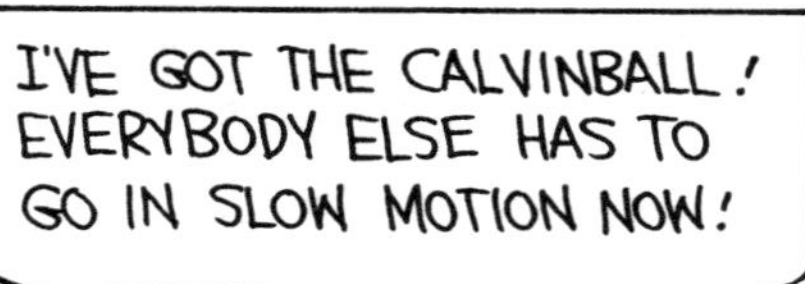

I'VE GOT THE CALVINBALL! EVERYBODY ELSE HAS TO GO IN SLOW MOTION NOW!

WAIT A MINUTE, CALVIN. I DON'T...
YOU HAVE TO **TALK** IN SLOW MOTION TOO. LIIIKE THISSS.

THIISSS GAAAAME MAAAKES NOOOO SENNNSE! IT'SSSS AASSS IFFFF YOU'RRRRE MAAAKINNNGGG IIIIIT UUUUP AAAS YOUUU GOOO.

HOBBES! SHE STUMBLED INTO THE PERIMETER OF WISDOM! RUN!!
OH...

IF I'M IN THE PERIMETER OF WISDOM, THEN I GET TO MAKE A DECREE.
A DECREE? UM.. OK.
I DECREE YOU HAVE TO CATCH A WATER BALLOON THAT I THROW HIGH IN THE AIR.
OH **NO**!

MAN, SHE PICKED UP THE NUANCES OF THIS GAME **FAST**!
HA! THIS **IS** FUN!
WATTERSON

OK CALVIN, YOU HAVE TO CATCH THE WATER BALLOON!
AAA!

HA! I'M IN THE COROLLARY ZONE! IF I CATCH THE BALLOON, THE THROWER HAS TO BEND OVER AND HOLD STILL!
WHAT?!

I CAUGHT IT!! HA HA HA HA!

OH THIS IS GOING TO BE **SWEET**!
I'M TAKING HOBBES PRISONER!
WATTERSON

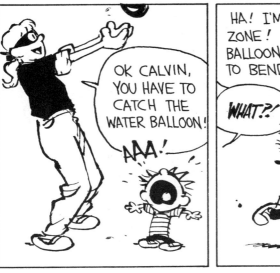

HOBBES! DON'T GUARD ROSALYN! I'M GOING TO GET HER WITH THIS BALLOON!
THE TIGER IS MY PRISONER!
I GUESS I'LL JUST HAVE TO SOAK YOU **BOTH** THEN! HA HA HA!
SORRY, CALVIN, I TOUCHED YOU WITH THE BABY SITTER FLAG.
THE BABY SITTER FLAG ?? WHAT'S THAT?
IT MEANS YOU MUST OBEY THE BABY SITTER.
...WHO SAYS IT'S A HALF-HOUR PAST YOUR BEDTIME NOW. LET'S GO IN.
AWWWWW! DARN BABY SITTER FLAG.
WATTERSON
OUR HOUSE IS STILL STANDING. THAT'S A GOOD SIGN.
WE'RE HOME! IS EVERYTHING OK?
FINE.
CALVIN DID HIS HOMEWORK, THEN WE PLAYED A GAME, AND CALVIN WENT TO BED.
IT'S AWFULLY LATE FOR JOKES, ROSALYN.
I'VE NOTICED THAT WHEN WE PLAY GAMES WITH GIRLS, YOU GET CAPTURED A LOT.
SOME OF US ARE JUST IRRESISTIBLE.
WATTERSON

Calvin and Hobbes
by Watterson
THE BIG, STUPID ULTRASAUR TAKES A LONG DRINK...
..A VERY LONG DRINK!
THE FEROCIOUS ALLOSAUR IS THIRSTY TOO! THIS MEANS CONFRONTATION!
..AH HEH HEH..
FORTUNATELY, THIS ALLOSAUR IS THE PATIENT TYPE.
Don't make me smack you across the hall, twerp.

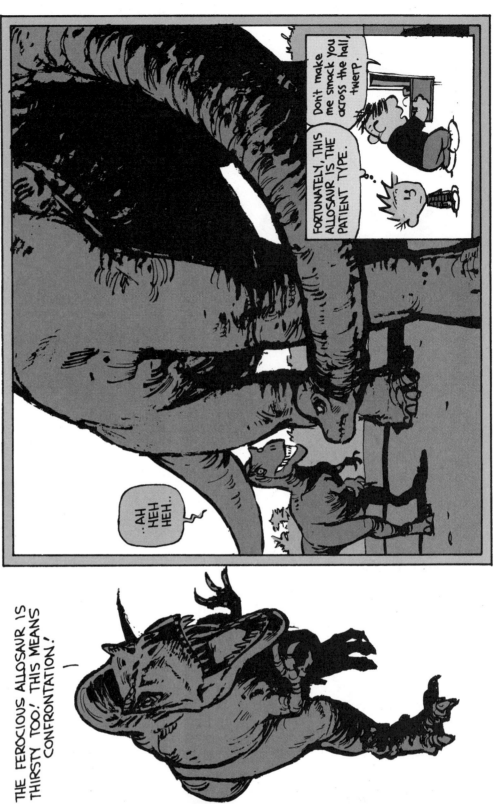

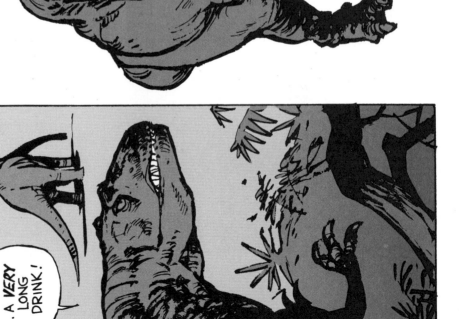

WAKE UP! IT'S TIME TO GET READY FOR SCHOOL.
UHNGGG

JUST CHECKING. I'M GLAD YOU'RE UP AND DRESSED.

THAT SHOULD THROW HER OFF THE TRAIL FOR A WHILE.
WATTERSON

FOR SHOW AND TELL, I BROUGHT A LITTLE TOY AIRPLANE.

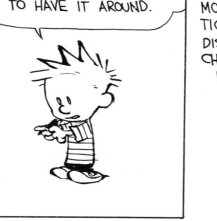

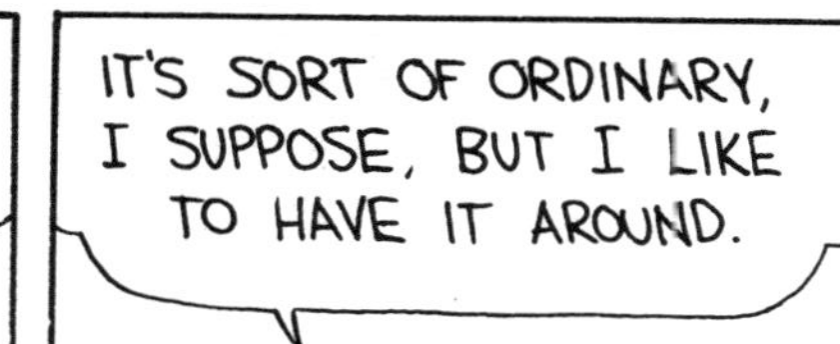
IT'S SORT OF ORDINARY, I SUPPOSE, BUT I LIKE TO HAVE IT AROUND.

IT REMINDS ME THAT AS SOON AS I SAVE A LITTLE MORE MONEY, I'LL BUY A TICKET AND PUT SO MUCH DISTANCE BETWEEN YOU CHUMPS AND ME, IT WILL BOGGLE YOUR MINDS!

IT'S NOT AN "ATTITUDE," IT'S A FACT!
WATTERSON

CALVIN AND HOBBES by WATTERSON
I HATE SUNDAYS. THE DAY OFF IS RUINED BY KNOWING I'VE GOT TO GET READY FOR SCHOOL TOMORROW.

WHY DON'T WE GET YOUR CHORES DONE NOW, SO WE CAN ENJOY THE REST OF THE DAY WITHOUT WORRY?

HMM.. I HATE TO DELAY FUN, BUT MAYBE YOU'RE ON TO SOMETHING.
THIS WILL MAKE THE FUN MORE FUN.

AT LAST! WE GOT EVERYTHING BAD OUT OF THE WAY!

THERE YOU ARE. IT'S TIME FOR BED.

SEE IF I EVER LISTEN TO YOU AGAIN!
NEVER PUT THE LOW PRIORITIES FIRST.

"ORIGINAL FLAVOR"... WAIT, HERE'S "LESS SODIUM," AND HERE'S "LITE," AND HERE'S "LESS FAT."

WHAT IF I WANT LESS FAT **AND** LESS SALT? WHAT DISTINGUISHES "LITE" FROM THESE OTHERS? DOES THE "ORIGINAL FLAVOR" PACKAGE IMPLY THAT THE OTHERS TASTE DIFFERENT?

FRANKLY, MY LIFE WAS PLENTY COMPLICATED **BEFORE** THE POTATO CHIPS.
WATTERSON

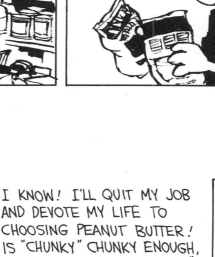

LOOK AT ALL THIS PEANUT BUTTER! THERE MUST BE THREE SIZES OF FIVE BRANDS OF FOUR CONSISTENCIES! WHO DEMANDS THIS MUCH CHOICE ?!?

I KNOW! I'LL QUIT MY JOB AND DEVOTE MY LIFE TO CHOOSING PEANUT BUTTER! IS "CHUNKY" CHUNKY ENOUGH, OR DO I NEED "**EXTRA** CHUNKY"?

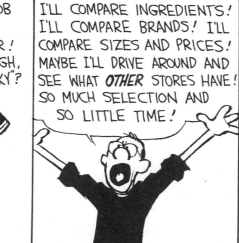

I'LL COMPARE INGREDIENTS! I'LL COMPARE BRANDS! I'LL COMPARE SIZES AND PRICES! MAYBE I'LL DRIVE AROUND AND SEE WHAT **OTHER** STORES HAVE! SO MUCH SELECTION AND SO LITTLE TIME!

I THINK **YOU** SHOULD DO THE SHOPPING.
DID THE MANAGER HAVE TO TALK TO YOU AGAIN?
HEY, WHERE'S THE PEANUT BUTTER ?!
WATTERSON

OOK OOK EE! OOH! OOK
!
IN HUMOR, TIMING IS EVERYTHING.
WATTERSON

I LIKE CEREAL TO CRACKLE AND POP WHEN I PUT MILK ON IT.
SEE? VERY ENTERTAINING!
I'VE NEVER SEEN RAISIN BRAN DO THAT.
I PUT IN AN ALKA-SELTZER.
WATTERSON

Calvin and Hobbes
by Watterson
THE CENTER SNAPS THE BALL TO THE QUARTERBACK!
NO HE DOESN'T!

HE DOESN'T?
NO! SECRETLY, HE'S THE QUARTERBACK FOR THE OTHER TEAM! HE KEEPS THE BALL!

A TRAITOR!
CALVIN BREAKS FOR THE GOAL!

WHEEEE! HE'S AT THE 30 ... THE 20... THE 10! NOBODY CAN CATCH HIM!
NOBODY WANTS TO! YOU'RE RUNNING TOWARD YOUR OWN GOAL!

HUH?!
WHEN I LEARNED YOU WERE A SPY, I SWITCHED GOALS. THIS IS YOUR GOAL AND MINE'S HIDDEN!

HIDDEN?!
YOU'LL NEVER FIND IT IN A MILLION YEARS!

I DON'T NEED TO FIND IT! AS A TRAITOR TO YOUR TEAM, CROSSING MY GOAL COUNTS AS CROSSING YOUR GOAL!
AH, YOU MIGHT THINK SO...

IN FACT, I KNOW SO!
BUT THE PLACE I HID MY GOAL IS RIGHT ON TOP OF YOUR GOAL, SO THE POINTS WILL GO TO ME!

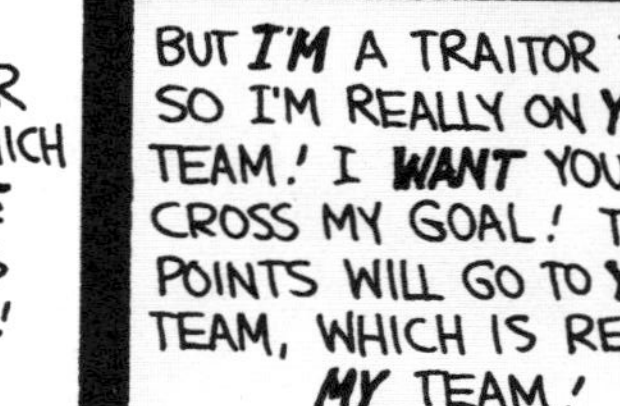
BUT THE FACT IS, I'M REALLY A DOUBLE AGENT! I'M ON YOUR TEAM AFTER ALL, WHICH MEANS YOU'LL LOSE POINTS IF I CROSS YOUR GOAL! HA HA!

BUT I'M A TRAITOR TOO, SO I'M REALLY ON YOUR TEAM! I WANT YOU TO CROSS MY GOAL! THE POINTS WILL GO TO YOUR TEAM, WHICH IS REALLY MY TEAM!

THAT WOULD BE TRUE... IF I WERE A FOOTBALL PLAYER!
YOU MEAN..?

I'M ACTUALLY A BADMINTON PLAYER DISGUISED AS A DOUBLE-AGENT FOOTBALL PLAYER!!
AND I'M SECRETLY A VOLLEYBALL-CROQUET-POLO PLAYER!

SOONER OR LATER, ALL OUR GAMES TURN INTO CALVINBALL.
NO CHEATING!

I NEED YOUR HELP, HOBBES.
WHAT'S THE PROBLEM?
THE TEACHER SAID MY BOOK REPORT WAS TERRIBLE AND I NEED TO DO IT OVER.
REALLY??
OBVIOUSLY, I NEED A COOLER LETTERHEAD LOGO.
I'LL ADD MORE LANCE-TOTING TIGERS AROUND THE CALVIN SHIELD.
WATTERSON

I HEAR WE'RE HAVING A FIRE DRILL TODAY.
RIGHT.
WOW! HOW EXCITING! I CAN'T WAIT!
DO YOU KNOW WHAT TO DO?
YOU BET! WHEN DO THEY PASS OUT THE GASOLINE?
WATTERSON

AND SO, AFTER A THREE MINUTE DOWNPOUR, HE BECAME LUDICROUSLY ATTIRED FOR THE REST OF THE DAY.

NOT EVERYONE CAN GET A FULL ISOMETRIC WORKOUT JUST BY YAWNING.

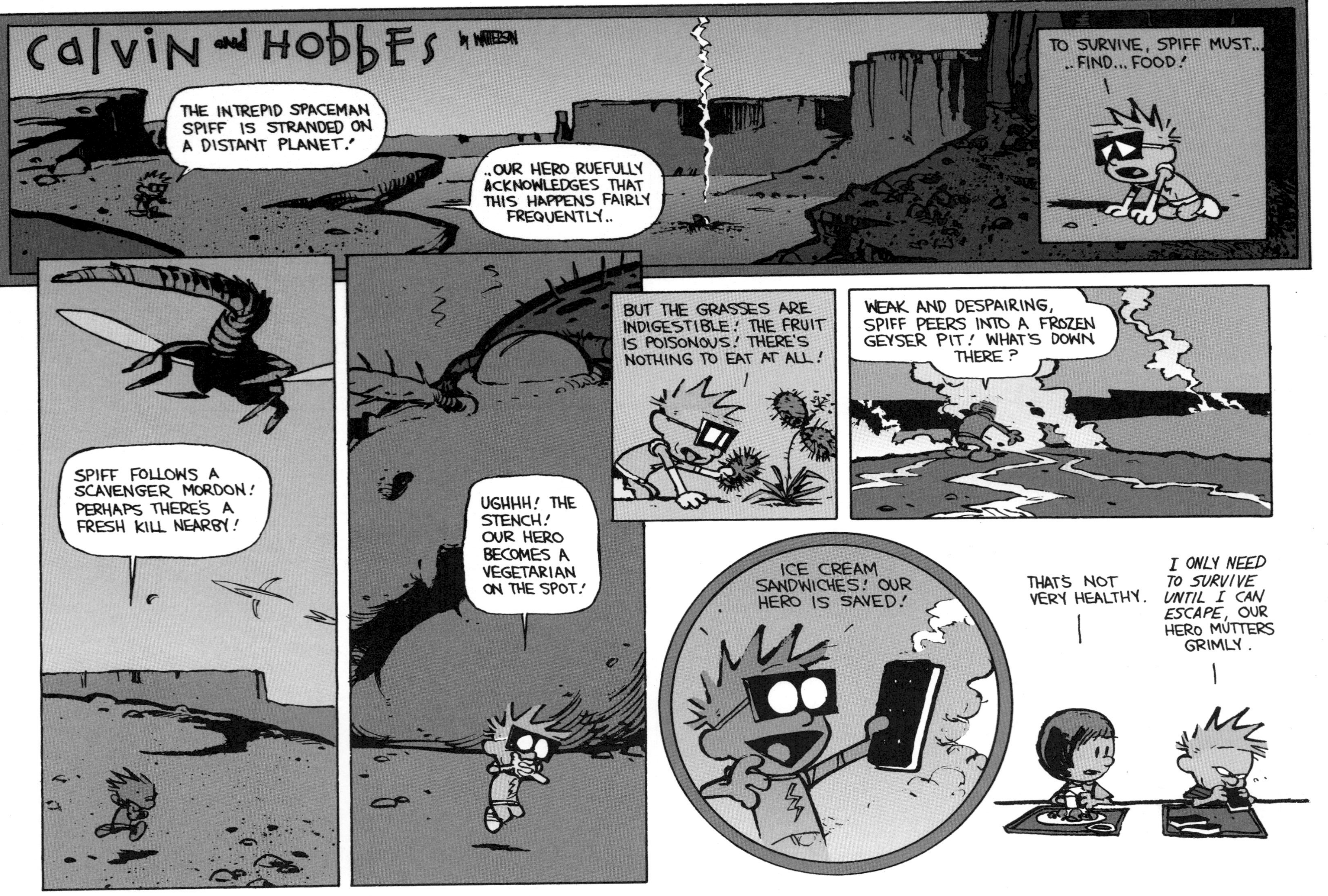
Calvin and Hobbes
by WATTERSON
THE INTREPID SPACEMAN SPIFF IS STRANDED ON A DISTANT PLANET!
..OUR HERO RUEFULLY ACKNOWLEDGES THAT THIS HAPPENS FAIRLY FREQUENTLY..
TO SURVIVE, SPIFF MUST.. ..FIND... FOOD!
SPIFF FOLLOWS A SCAVENGER MORDON! PERHAPS THERE'S A FRESH KILL NEARBY!
UGHHH! THE STENCH! OUR HERO BECOMES A VEGETARIAN ON THE SPOT!
BUT THE GRASSES ARE INDIGESTIBLE! THE FRUIT IS POISONOUS! THERE'S NOTHING TO EAT AT ALL!
WEAK AND DESPAIRING, SPIFF PEERS INTO A FROZEN GEYSER PIT! WHAT'S DOWN THERE?
ICE CREAM SANDWICHES! OUR HERO IS SAVED!
THAT'S NOT VERY HEALTHY.
I ONLY NEED TO SURVIVE UNTIL I CAN ESCAPE, OUR HERO MUTTERS GRIMLY.

I WISH SCHOOL WOULD DISAPPEAR FOREVER, RIGHT NOW!

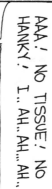

!

TO MAKE A BAD DAY WORSE, SPEND IT WISHING FOR THE IMPOSSIBLE.

UH OH, I FEEL A SNEEZE COMING ON.

AAA! NO TISSUE! NO HANKY! I.. AH.. AH... AH..

KACHOO!

OF MY LIMITED OPTIONS, THIS WAS PROBABLY THE WORST.

Calvin and Hobbes by WATTERSON

5
+3
421
38.

THE WORLD ISN'T SO BAD IF YOU CAN JUST GET OUT IN IT.

BOY, I HATE SCHOOL ASSIGNMENTS! MISS WORMWOOD IS OUT TO DESTROY MY LIFE!

WHAT DO YOU HAVE TO DO?
MAKE A LEAF COLLECTION! WHAT A DUMB WASTE OF TIME!

HOW MANY LEAVES DO YOU NEED?
50! I GOTTA COLLECT 50 LEAVES!

AND JUST WHEN I THOUGHT OF A LOOPHOLE, THE TEACHER SAID EVERY LEAF HAS TO BE A DIFFERENT KIND.
SHE'S GOT YOUR NUMBER.
WHEN DO YOU NEED TO PRESENT YOUR LEAF COLLECTION?
IN TWO WEEKS.

THAT'S NOT SO BAD. YOU JUST NEED THREE OR FOUR LEAVES A DAY.
I'M NOT WORKING ON WEEKENDS.

OK, FIVE LEAVES A DAY.
AND MY WEEKDAYS ARE BOOKED UNTIL NEXT THURSDAY AT 6 PM!

SO YOU NEED 50 LEAVES AN HOUR.
SEE?? IT'S IMPOSSIBLE!

HERE'S A NICE LEAF! DO YOU WANT IT FOR YOUR COLLECTION?
NO.
WHY NOT?
IT'S A BEAUTIFUL AFTERNOON! I'M NOT GOING TO WASTE IT DOING RIDICULOUS BUSYWORK FOR SCHOOL!
BUT THIS WOULD BE ONE LESS LEAF YOU'D NEED TO COLLECT LATER.
YEAH, BUT IT'S ONE **MORE** LEAF THAN I NEED RIGHT NOW.
SOMEHOW, IT'S ALWAYS RIGHT NOW UNTIL IT'S LATER.
WHATEVER ***THAT*** MEANS.

OUR LEAF COLLECTIONS AREN'T DUE FOR A WEEK YET! HOW COULD YOU POSSIBLY BE ALMOST DONE ?!

I MAKE IT A GAME. I PRETEND IT'S A CONTEST TO SEE HOW MANY LEAVES I CAN FIND EACH DAY. THAT WAY, IT'S NOT AN ASSIGNMENT, IT'S FUN!

DID YOU KNOW THAT'S ONE OF THE TEN WARNING SIGNS OF HOPELESS DWEEBISM?
I'LL BET ANOTHER SIGN IS MOVING TO THE NEXT GRADE EACH YEAR.

THE TEACHER REMINDED US THAT WE ONLY HAVE A WEEK LEFT TO FINISH OUR LEAF COLLECTIONS, SO WE OUGHT TO BE HALF DONE NOW.

YOU HAVEN'T EVEN STARTED.
YEAH, BUT I WORK BETTER UNDER PRESSURE.

ACTUALLY, YOU WORK **ONLY** UNDER PRESSURE.
THAT WAY, THE WORK TIME IS MORE MISERABLE, BUT THERE'S LESS OF IT.

MOM, I NEED TO COLLECT LEAVES FOR A SCHOOL PROJECT. COULD WE GO TO THE ARBORETUM SOMETIME?
SURE. HOW ABOUT THIS WEEKEND?
UM, IT WOULD BE BETTER TO DO IT A LITTLE SOONER.
WHEN IS THIS DUE?
WELL, MY NOTEBOOK'S IN THE CAR AND THE PARK CLOSES IN 20 MINUTES.
CALVIN, I'M FIXING DINNER!

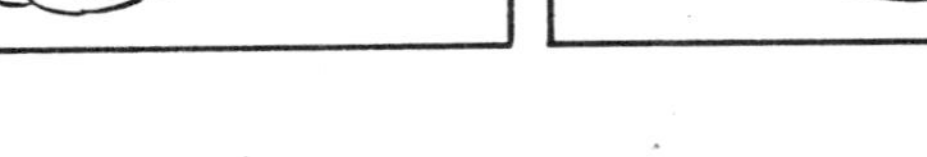
MY LEAF COLLECTION IS DOOMED! I CAN'T BELIEVE MOM WOULDN'T TAKE ME TO THE ARBORETUM. NO WONDER I GET BAD GRADES!

WELL, YOU DID SPRING THE IDEA ON HER AT THE LAST SECOND..
THAT'S WHEN I THOUGHT OF IT! THE PROBLEM IS THAT MOM'S NOT FLEXIBLE.
WHAT A STUPID WASTE OF TIME THIS IS! I WISH THERE WAS SOME WAY OUT OF THIS ASSIGNMENT.

WUMMWUMMWU
MWUM

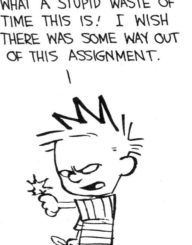

A UFO!!
TAKE US TO THE SUPREME EARTHLING POTENTATE.
UM... WELL..
SPEAKING.
AH! WHAT LUCK.
IT WAS I WHO CHOSE THE LANDING SITE. KUDOS FOR NAVIGATOR NEBULAR!
WATTERSON

SO, UH, WHAT CAN I DO FOR YOU?
WE ARE TAKING OVER YOUR WORLD.
YOU ARE?? WHAT FOR??
EARTH IS PRIME REAL ESTATE.
LOCATION, LOCATION, LOCATION.
I GUESS I'D NEVER THOUGHT ABOUT THAT.
CHARM, ATMOSPHERE, QUIET GALAXY...
ACTUALLY, THE ATMOSPHERE NEEDS CLEANING.
A. GOOD FIXER UPPER.
WATTERSON

AND BEST OF ALL, NOW WE DON'T NEED TO WASTE ANY MORE TIME ON THIS! THE ALIENS ARE DOING ALL THE WORK! WE CAN GOOF OFF THE REST OF THE DAY!

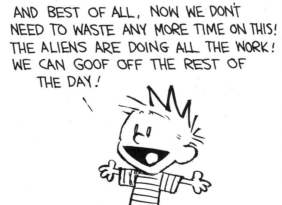

HEY, NO TV UNTIL YOUR LEAF COLLECTION IS DONE.
IT'S GETTING DONE AS WE SPEAK.
WHAT'S THAT SUPPOSED TO MEAN? LET'S SEE IT.
I CAN'T SHOW YOU UNTIL LATER TONIGHT.
WHY NOT?
YOU SHOULD PROBABLY SIT DOWN.
MAN, SHE DIDN'T EVEN WANT TO **HEAR** ABOUT IT.

IT'S ALMOST BEDTIME AND THE ALIENS HAVEN'T COME BACK WITH THE LEAVES.
IT'S A LONG TRIP.
WHAT IF THEY DON'T SHOW UP?
THEY **SAID** THEY WOULD.
MAYBE THEY GOT LOST.
SPACE ALIENS DON'T GET LOST! THEY'VE GOT SUPERIOR TECHNOLOGY! EVERYBODY KNOWS THAT!
IT'S A BIG UNIVERSE.
I'LL TURN ON SOME MORE LIGHTS.

THE ALIENS STILL HAVEN'T SHOWN UP! WHAT ARE WE GOING TO DO?? I'VE GOT TO TURN IN MY LEAF COLLECTION TOMORROW!

I'LL BET THOSE DUMB ALIENS GOT BACK TO THEIR PLANET AND PROCRASTINATED! I'LL BET THEY HAVE NO RESPECT FOR DEADLINES! I'LL BET THEY PUT EVERYTHING OFF AND ARE DOING A LOUSY JOB AT THE LAST SECOND!

HOW COULD ANYONE BE SO IRRESPONSIBLE?
IF THEY'RE NOT HERE IN FIVE MINUTES, I'M NOT HANDING OVER THE EARTH! THEY'VE GOT TO LEARN A LESSON!

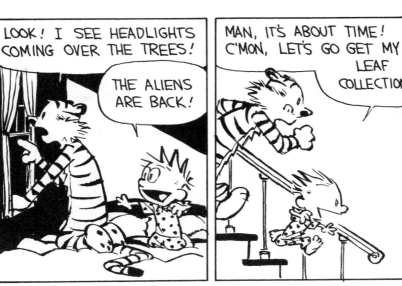

LOOK! I SEE HEADLIGHTS COMING OVER THE TREES!

THE ALIENS ARE BACK!

MAN, IT'S ABOUT TIME! C'MON, LET'S GO GET MY LEAF COLLECTION!

YOU'RE OUT COLLECTING **LEAVES** AT **THIS** HOUR IN YOUR **PAJAMAS**?!? GET BACK IN BED!!
I **TOLD** YOU! SPACE ALIENS GAVE ME THESE! THEY JUST LEFT!

BOY, YOU LOOK TIRED. I'LL BET YOU WERE UP LATE DOING YOUR LEAF COLLECTION.

MAYBE, BUT **I'VE** GOT THE BEST COLLECTION OF ALL! **MY** LEAVES ARE FROM ANOTHER PLANET!
WHAT?!

SEE HOW BIZARRE THEY ARE? THE LABELS ARE EVEN WRITTEN IN AN ALIEN LANGUAGE! LOOK AT THEIR COOL ALPHABET!

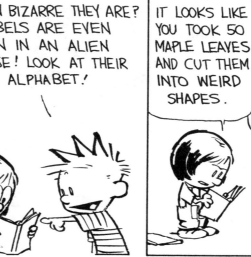

IT LOOKS LIKE YOU TOOK 50 MAPLE LEAVES AND CUT THEM INTO WEIRD SHAPES.
ALIENS NOW OWN THE EARTH AND I TOLD THEM GIRLS MAKE GOOD ZOO EXHIBITS.

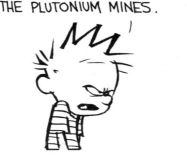

THE TEACHER DIDN'T BELIEVE MY LEAVES WERE FROM AN ALIEN PLANET.

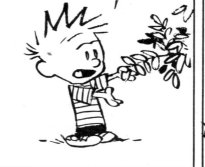

SHE SAID IT WAS OBVIOUS I DID THE WHOLE THING LAST NIGHT AND I MADE A MOCKERY OF THE ASSIGNMENT. WELL, SHE'LL BE SORRY WHEN THE ALIENS SEND HER TO THE PLUTONIUM MINES.

SHE JUST WON'T ADMIT IT WAS A POINTLESS PROJECT. WHO CARES ABOUT LEAVES?! WHAT USELESS KNOWLEDGE!

I BELIEVE THAT'S POISON SUMAC YOU'RE HOLDING.
THIS?? WHAT MAKES YOU SAY THAT?

calvin and HobbEs
by WATTERSON
I LOVE FALL.
I LIKE THE COOL DAYS, THE SMELL OF LEAVES, THE LOW SUNLIGHT... AND THE SKY LOOKS EVEN MORE BLUE WHEN THE TREES ARE YELLOW AND RED!
I DUNNO... I THINK AUTUMN IS MELANCHOLY. SUMMER IS OVER AND IN A WEEK OR TWO, EVERYTHING WILL BE HUNKERED DOWN FOR THE LONG, BLEAK WINTER.
NOTHING LASTS. FALL IS JUST THE LAST FLING BEFORE THINGS GET WORSE.
IF GOOD THINGS LASTED FOREVER, WOULD WE APPRECIATE HOW PRECIOUS THEY ARE?
I LIKE TO HAVE EVERYTHING SO GOOD, I CAN TAKE IT ALL FOR GRANTED.
I THINK THE BRISK AIR MAKES APPLE PIE TASTE BETTER TOO! MM-MM!

HE'S AT THE 30... THE 20... CALVIN'S GOING FOR THE TOUCHDOWN!

WAAA
THWANGG

YOU'RE SUPPOSED TO *TACKLE* ME!
I DUNNO... THAT SEEMS SO LOWBROW.

calvin and HobbES by WATTERSON

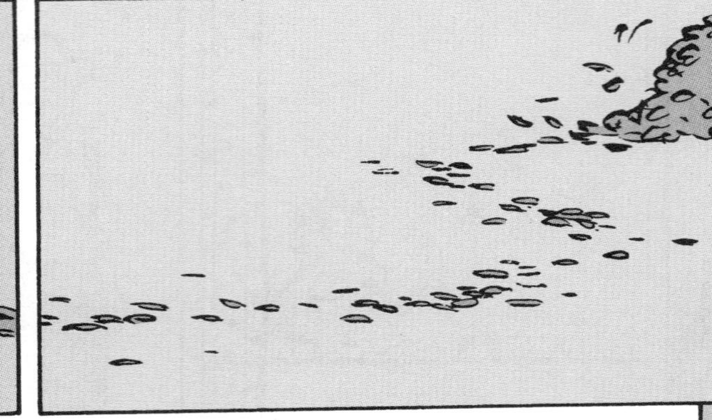

YOU KNOW, SCHOOL WOULDN'T BE SO BAD IF YOU DIDN'T HAVE TO GO EVERY DAY.

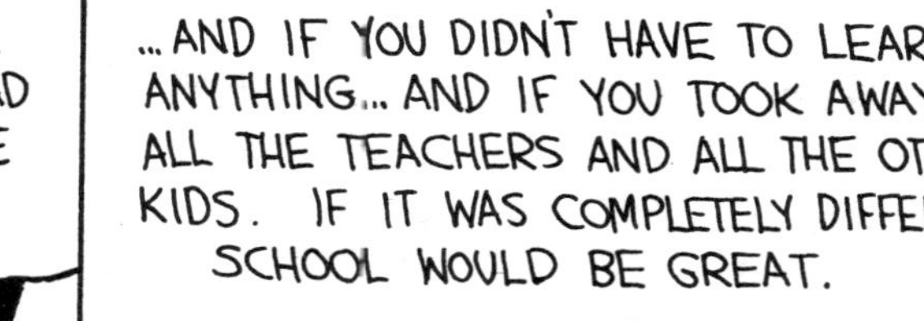
...AND IF YOU DIDN'T HAVE TO LEARN ANYTHING... AND IF YOU TOOK AWAY ALL THE TEACHERS AND ALL THE OTHER KIDS. IF IT WAS COMPLETELY DIFFERENT, SCHOOL WOULD BE GREAT.

A LOT OF THINGS ARE LIKE THAT.
NOBODY ASKS ME HOW THINGS OUGHT TO BE. I'VE GOT TONS OF IDEAS!

YES, CALVIN?
HEY KIDS, ON TOMORROW'S SHOW AND TELL, I'LL BE BRINGING A BIG SURPRISE! WILL IT SHOCK AND AMAZE YOU... **OR** WILL IT DISGUST AND TERRIFY YOU?!? FIND OUT TOMORROW WHEN I REVEAL MY NEXT ***SHOW AND TELL*** *HORROR*! DON'T MISS IT!

RETURNING TO THE ***LESSON***...
THAT'S CALLED A TEASER, BY THE WAY.

IN THE FUTURE, EVERYTHING WILL BE EFFORTLESS!

COMPUTERS WILL TAKE CARE OF EVERY TASK. WE'LL JUST POINT TO WHAT WE WANT DONE AND CLICK. WE'LL NEVER NEED TO LEAVE THE CLIMATE-CONTROLLED COMFORT OF OUR HOMES!
NO NUISANCE, NO WASTED TIME, NO ANNOYING HUMAN INTERACTION...
...NO LIFE.
LIFE IS TOO INCONVENIENT.

YOU'RE GOING TO JUGGLE EGGS?
IT'S A METAPHOR FOR LIFE, HOBBES.
EACH EGG REPRESENTS ONE OF LIFE'S CONCERNS AND THE GOAL IS TO GIVE EACH THE APPROPRIATE AMOUNT OF INDIVIDUAL ATTENTION WHILE SIMULTANEOUSLY WATCHING AND GUIDING ALL THE OTHERS.
LIFE IS ABOUT BALANCE AND STAYING QUICK AND ALERT AS EVERYTHING THREATENS TO SPIN OUT OF CONTROL!

AND SOMETIMES WE MAKE A BIG MESS OF THINGS.
BUT THE IMPORTANT THING IS PERSISTENCE.

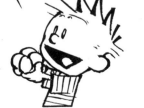

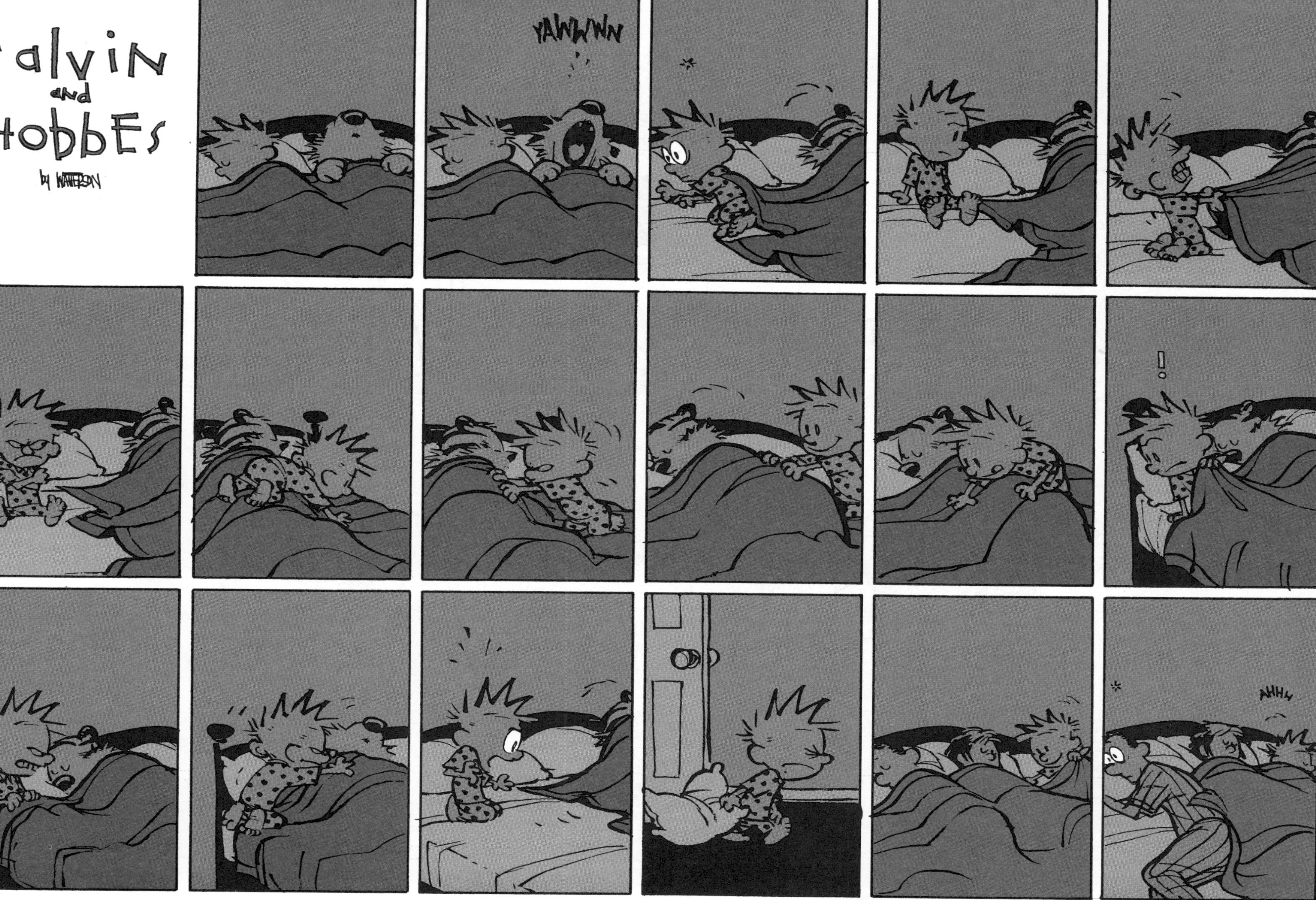
Calvin and Hobbes
by WATTERSON
YAWWWN
!
AHHH

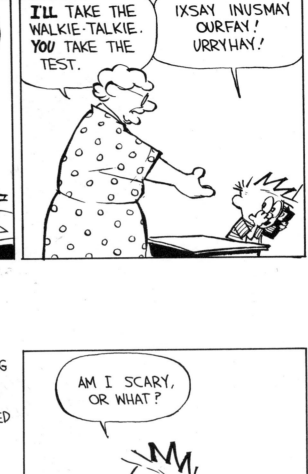

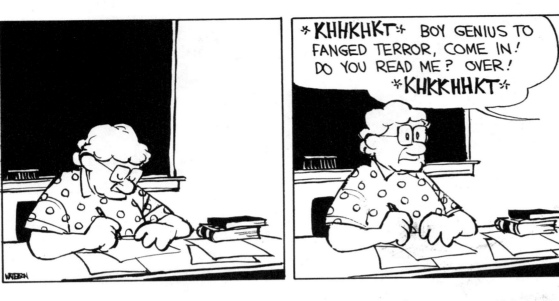

KHHKHKT BOY GENIUS TO FANGED TERROR, COME IN! DO YOU READ ME? OVER! *KHKKHHKT*
I'LL TAKE THE WALKIE-TALKIE. **YOU** TAKE THE TEST.
IXSAY INUSMAY OURFAY! URRYHAY!

TRICK OR TREAT!
WHERE'S YOUR COSTUME? WHAT ARE YOU SUPPOSED TO BE?

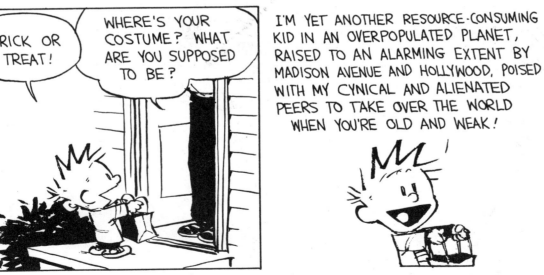

I'M YET ANOTHER RESOURCE-CONSUMING KID IN AN OVERPOPULATED PLANET, RAISED TO AN ALARMING EXTENT BY MADISON AVENUE AND HOLLYWOOD, POISED WITH MY CYNICAL AND ALIENATED PEERS TO TAKE OVER THE WORLD WHEN YOU'RE OLD AND WEAK!

AM I SCARY, OR WHAT?

BOK

WHIFF
WHAFF
FIFF
FOOF

I CAN'T HELP BUT WONDER WHAT KIND OF DESPERATE STRAITS WOULD DRIVE A MAN TO INVENT THIS THING.

LOOK! GEESE FLYING SOUTH FOR THE WINTER.

TWICE A YEAR THEY MIGRATE THOUSANDS OF MILES ACROSS THE CONTINENT IN AN EXHAUSTING, ETERNAL STRUGGLE TO FULFILL NATURE'S UNYIELDING DEMANDS!

I'LL BET THAT GETS OLD REAL FAST.
YOU DON'T SEE **ME** KEEPING A SUMMER HOME.

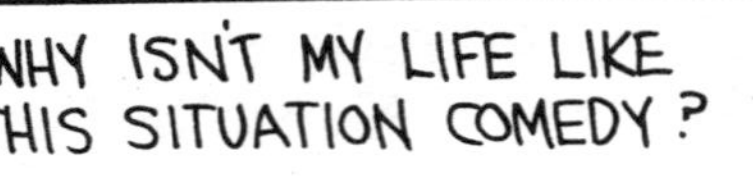

WHY ISN'T MY LIFE LIKE THIS SITUATION COMEDY?

WHY DON'T I HAVE A BUNCH OF FRIENDS WITH NOTHING TO DO BUT DROP BY AND INSTIGATE WACKY ADVENTURES?

WHY AREN'T MY CONVERSATIONS PEPPERED WITH SPONTANEOUS WITTICISMS? WHY DON'T MY FRIENDS DEMONSTRATE HEARTFELT CONCERN FOR MY WELL-BEING WHEN I HAVE PROBLEMS?

WHY DON'T YOU KNOW ANY GORGEOUS BABES?
I GOTTA GET MY LIFE SOME WRITERS.

KNOW WHAT'S WEIRD? DAY BY DAY NOTHING SEEMS TO CHANGE, BUT PRETTY SOON, EVERYTHING IS DIFFERENT.

YOU JUST GO ABOUT YOUR BUSINESS AND ONE DAY YOU REALIZE YOU'RE NOT THE SAME PERSON YOU USED TO BE. PEOPLE CHANGE WHETHER THEY DECIDE TO OR NOT!

THANK HEAVEN FOR SMALL FAVORS.

FOR EXAMPLE, I USED TO BE MORE TOLERANT OF OBLIQUE ASPERSIONS.

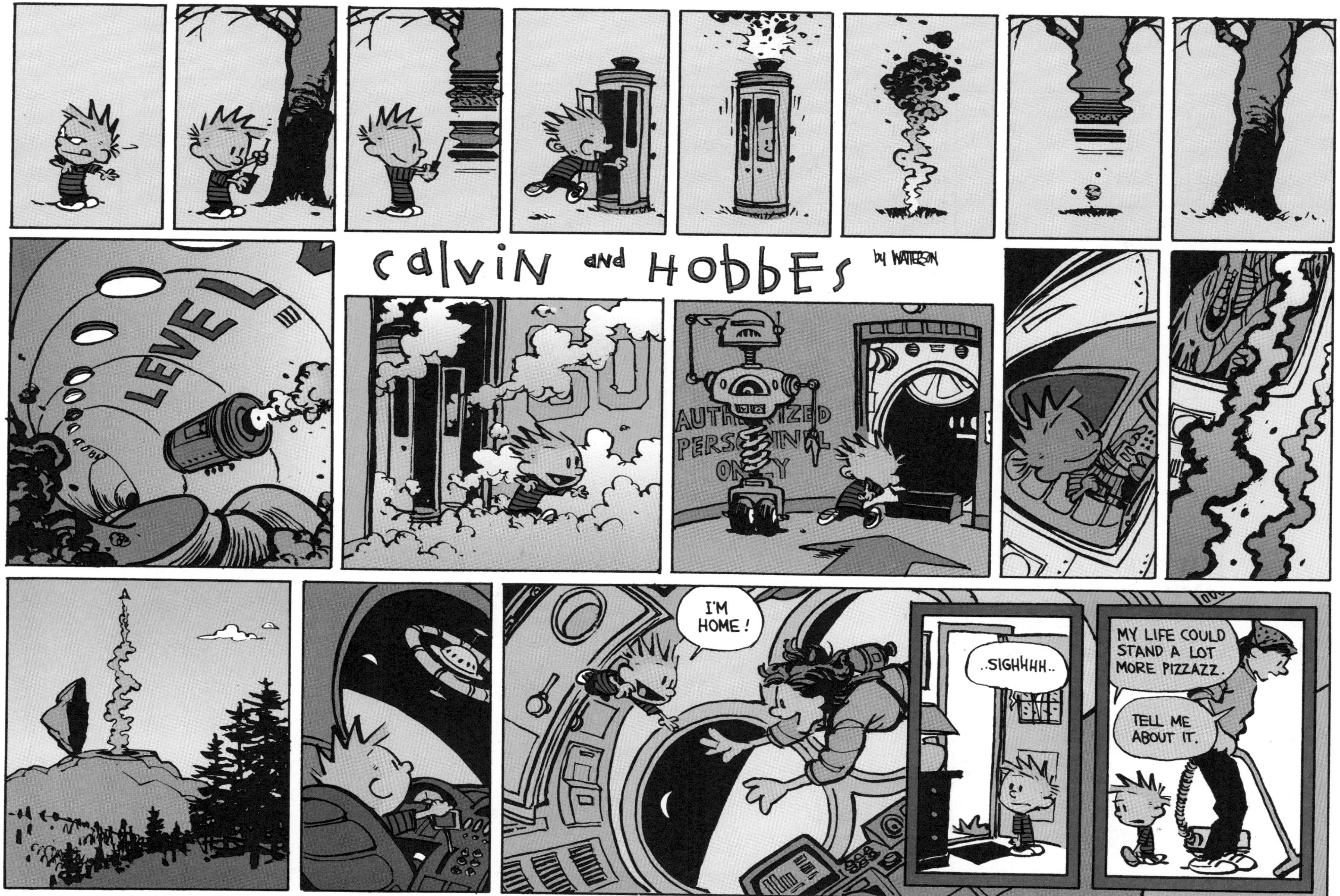

Calvin and Hobbes by WATTERSON

I'M HOME!

..SIGHHHH..

MY LIFE COULD STAND A LOT MORE PIZZAZZ.

TELL ME ABOUT IT.

I WONDER HOW LONG IT'S BEEN SINCE I LAST LOOKED AT THE CLOCK. MAYBE IT'S BEEN AN HOUR.
WELL, ACTUALLY IT'S PROBABLY BEEN ONLY 40 MINUTES. I'LL GUESS HALF AN HOUR TO BE SAFE.
20 SECONDS ?!?
IT'S GOING TO BE A VERY BAD DAY.
CALVIN, SIT UP.
WATTERSON

I'M IN A VERY CRABBY MOOD, SO EVERYBODY JUST LEAVE ME ALONE! I HATE EVERYONE!!
NOBODY RECOGNIZES MY HINTS TO SMOTHER ME WITH AFFECTION.
WATTERSON

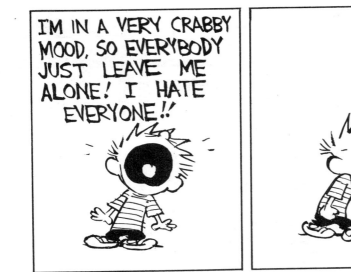

AS A GENIUS, IT'S IMPORTANT THAT I WRITE A LOT OF LETTERS.

AFTER ALL, MY CORRESPONDENCE WILL BE THE BASIC RESOURCE MATERIAL FOR HISTORIANS TO RECONSTRUCT MY LIFE. MY WRITING WILL PROVIDE COUNTLESS FASCINATING INSIGHTS FOR BIOGRAPHERS.

SUCH AS HOW ALL YOUR SALUTATIONS BEGIN, "HEY BOOGERBRAIN."
IT'S BEEN THREE WEEKS AND I STILL HAVEN'T RECEIVED MY X-RAY GLASSES!

YIKES! NOT ANOTHER EXTREME CLOSE-UP ON SOMEBODY'S ANGUISH AND GRIEF!
WHY DO TV CAMERAS ZOOM IN SO CLOSE TO PEOPLE'S FACES THAT YOU CAN'T EVEN SEE THEIR ENTIRE HEADS?! DO THEY THINK WE CAN'T READ THE PERSON'S EXPRESSION FROM MORE THAN TWO INCHES AWAY?!
WHAT A VIOLATION OF PERSONAL SPACE! WHAT A SHAMELESS INTRUSION! WHAT A HEARTLESS ASSAULT ON HUMAN DIGNITY!

WHY ARE YOU STANDING AGAINST THE WALL?
I'M WATCHING TV.

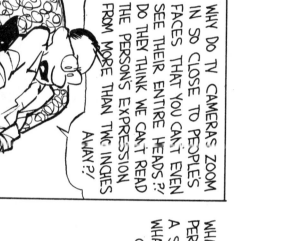

AUGHH! THIS STUPID TOASTER BURNED MY TOAST!!

LOOK AT THIS! MY TOAST IS CHARRED TO A BLACK CINDER! I CAN'T EAT THIS! IT'S RUINED! RUINED!!

SO STICK IN ANOTHER PIECE OF BREAD AND WATCH IT THIS TIME.

ARE YOU SUGGESTING THAT THIS APPLIANCE DIDN'T AGGRAVATE ME WITH MALICE AFORETHOUGHT?!

I KEEP HAVING THE SAME WEIRD DREAM EVERY NIGHT.

IF IT'S THE SAME DREAM, IT MUST MEAN SOMETHING.

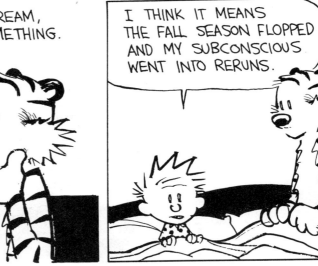

I THINK IT MEANS THE FALL SEASON FLOPPED AND MY SUBCONSCIOUS WENT INTO RERUNS.

"OPERATION KAPOW!" (CALVIN: GENIUS + MASTERMIND; HOBBES: CREATIVE CONSULTANT + CARTOGRAPHER)
TOP SECRET!! DO NOT READ THIS!! THIS MEANS YOU!
#1: TAKE SLED TO TOP OF MT. VERTIGO
#2: GET UP SPEED
FASTER FASTER!
(THIS SHOULD LOOK STEEPER)
(TREES→)
#3: NAVIGATE THROUGH WOODS (IN CASE ENEMIES ARE FOLLOWING)
WHEW
#4: GO TO SECRET PINE TREE
#5: GRAB HIDDEN BUCKET OF SNOWBALLS!
KAPOW!
I HATE YOU CALVIN OW OW OW OW OW!
#6: BLAST SUSIE! HA HA!
UHH YOU WIN
WHEEE
#7: MAKE GETAWAY (GO FAST HERE)
#8: HIT RAMP
DEEP TRENCH
#9: HIDE IN IMPENETRABLE FORTRESS. PLOT NEXT ATTACK!
MEDAL OF SUCCESS RECIPIENTS
(THIS FORT WILL BE REALLY REALLY BIG)
(5000 EXTRA SNOWBALLS)
DESTROY THIS MAP! CALVIN AND HOBBES = GREAT!!
CALVIN AND HOBBES by WATTERSON
NOW IF IT WOULD ONLY SNOW!
WHILE WE'RE WAITING, I'LL DRAW MORE SPIRALS ABOVE SUSIE'S HEAD.

BRRR, IT'S FREEZING OUT THERE! I DON'T WANT TO LEAVE MY NICE WARM BED.

ON DAYS LIKE THIS, I WISH MOM WOULD COME IN, LAY AN EXTRA BLANKET OVER ME, PAT MY HEAD, AND AS I SINK INTO THE PILLOW UNDER THE WEIGHT OF THE COVERS, SHE'D SAY...
HEY, LET'S MOVE IT!! THIS IS THE THIRD TIME I'VE CALLED YOU! YOU'RE GOING TO MISS THE BUS! LET'S GO!!
THESE MORNINGS ARE GOING TO KILL ME.
WATTERSON
THE PACE OF MODERN LIFE IS ALL WRONG. IT MAKES EVERY DAY AN ORDEAL. EVERYBODY'S EXHAUSTED, STRESSED OUT, AND SHORT-TEMPERED!

LOOK AT ME! WHY AM I WAITING FOR A BUS AT THIS HORRIBLE HOUR?! IT'S UNNATURAL AND UNHEALTHY!
WATTERSON
WE SHOULD EASE INTO THE DAY! YOU KNOW, READ THE PAPER, HAVE SOME HOT COCOA, GO FOR A LEISURELY WALK AND GET OUR THOUGHTS TOGETHER...
SO NOW IT'S MID-AFTERNOON.
RIGHT. TIME TO KICK BACK FOR A LITTLE SIESTA AND PLAN DINNER.

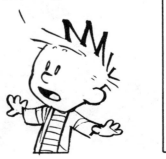

I WANT THE LAST PIECE OF PIE! DON'T DIVIDE IT UP! GIVE IT ALL TO ME!
DON'T BE SELFISH, CALVIN.
SO THE REAL MESSAGE HERE IS "BE DISHONEST"?
WATTERSON

UGGHH... MANICOTTI! GROSS!
SHLOOOP

AIEE! MY INTESTINES JUST BURST THROUGH MY STOMACH WALL!
AAAA!!
BLORK
I SHOULD GET SOME MORE AND SEE IF I CAN GET OUT OF MATH CLASS.
WATTERSON

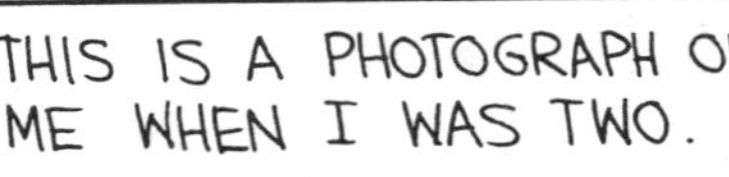

THIS IS A PHOTOGRAPH OF ME WHEN I WAS TWO.

IT'S STRANGE. I **KNOW** THAT'S ME, BUT I DON'T FEEL ANY CONNECTION TO THIS IMAGE. EVERYTHING IS SO DIFFERENT NOW.

ISN'T IT WEIRD THAT ONE'S OWN PAST CAN SEEM UNREAL? THIS IS LIKE LOOKING AT A PICTURE OF SOMEBODY ELSE.

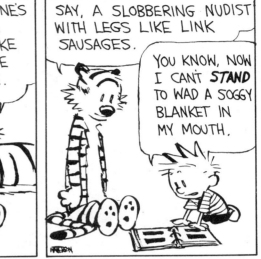

SAY, A SLOBBERING NUDIST WITH LEGS LIKE LINK SAUSAGES.
YOU KNOW, NOW I CAN'T **STAND** TO WAD A SOGGY BLANKET IN MY MOUTH.

HERE'S A PICTURE OF ME WHEN I WAS THREE. LOOK AT THAT SMILE!

AHH, THE ARROGANCE OF YOUTH! I THOUGHT I KNEW EVERYTHING WHEN I WAS THREE.

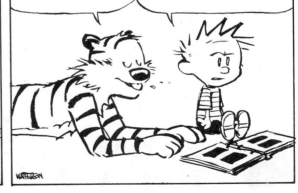

NOW, A LIFETIME OF EXPERIENCE HAS LEFT ME BITTER AND CYNICAL.
AND YOU EXPWETHED AWW THAT KNOWWEDGE WIKE THITH.

Calvin and Hobbes
by WATTERSON
Calvin

I'm gonna pound you at recess, Twinky.

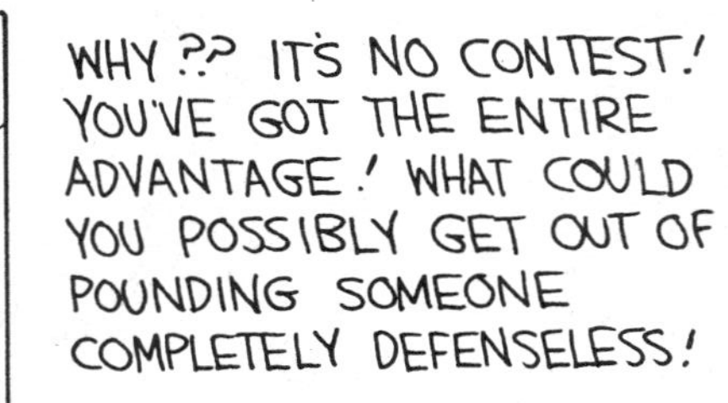
WHY ?? IT'S NO CONTEST! YOU'VE GOT THE ENTIRE ADVANTAGE! WHAT COULD YOU POSSIBLY GET OUT OF POUNDING SOMEONE COMPLETELY DEFENSELESS!

It's fun.
OH, HE'S A SPORTSMAN.

HELLO?
HI MOM, IT'S CALVIN.

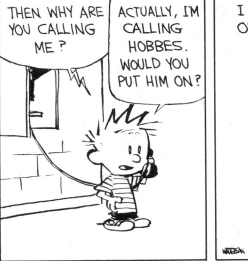

IS SOMETHING WRONG? YOU'RE SUPPOSED TO BE IN SCHOOL!
IT'S RECESS. I'M FINE.
THEN WHY ARE YOU CALLING ME?
ACTUALLY, I'M CALLING HOBBES. WOULD YOU PUT HIM ON?

I GOTTA GET MY OWN SECRETARY.

OOH, IT'S COLD TODAY! IT NEEDS TO BE 30 DEGREES WARMER OUT HERE!

FOR THAT MATTER, IT'S ALSO TOO QUIET. WE NEED SOME BACKGROUND MUSIC.

AND IT'S TOO SLOW! THINGS SHOULD HAPPEN MORE QUICKLY!

IF ONLY BEING OUTSIDE WERE MORE LIKE DRIVING A CAR.
YEAH, I COULD BE SITTING DOWN NOW TOO.

CALVIN, WILL YOU GATHER THE TRASH, PLEASE?
WHY SHOULD I? WHAT DO I GET IN RETURN?!

WE WILL FEED, CLOTHE, SHELTER, AND EDUCATE YOU THROUGHOUT YOUR ENTIRE YOUTH.

I REALLY HATE HAVING THINGS PUT IN PERSPECTIVE.

HOW COULD ANYONE WEAR OUT SHOES SO FAST?
I LEAD A RUGGED LIFE.
WATTERSON

I WISH IT WOULD SNOW!
!
I KNOW WHEN I'M BEING MOCKED.
WATTERSON

DOESN'T IT SEEM LIKE EVERYBODY JUST SHOUTS AT EACH OTHER NOWADAYS?
I THINK IT'S BECAUSE CONFLICT IS DRAMA, DRAMA IS ENTERTAINING, AND ENTERTAINMENT IS MARKETABLE.
FINDING CONSENSUS AND COMMON GROUND IS **DULL**! NOBODY WANTS TO WATCH A CIVILIZED DISCUSSION THAT ACKNOWLEDGES AMBIGUITY AND COMPLEXITY. WE WANT TO SEE FIREWORKS!
Calvin and Hobbes
by WATTERSON
WE WANT THE SENSE OF SOLIDARITY AND IDENTITY THAT COMES FROM HAVING OUR INTERESTS NARROWED AND EXPLOITED BY LIKE-MINDED ZEALOTS!
TALK SHOW HOSTS, POLITICAL CANDIDATES, NEWS PROGRAMS, SPECIAL INTEREST GROUPS... THEY ALL BECOME SUCCESSFUL BY REDUCING DEBATES TO THE LEVEL OF SHOUTED RAGE. NOTHING GETS SOLVED, BUT WE'RE ALL ENTERTAINED.
HMM, YOU MAY BE RIGHT.

WHAT A BORING DAY **THIS** TURNED OUT TO BE!

PEOPLE KEEP TALKING ABOUT OPENING MORE WILDERNESS FOR DEVELOPMENT.

WE SEEM TO UNDERSTAND THE VALUE OF OIL, TIMBER, MINERALS, AND HOUSING, BUT NOT THE VALUE OF UNSPOILED BEAUTY, WILDLIFE, SOLITUDE, AND SPIRITUAL RENEWAL.

WE NEED TO START PUTTING PRICES ON THE PRICELESS.
YEAH, IF OUR WOODS ARE WORTH A ZILLION JILLION BAGILLION, THINK WHAT ALASKA IS WORTH.
WATTERSON

IT'S FREEZING IN HERE!! WHY CAN'T WE CRANK UP THE THERMOSTAT?!

CONSUMING LESS FUEL IS BETTER FOR THE ENVIRONMENT AND IT SAVES MONEY.

OH.

..AND BEING COLD BUILDS CHARACTER.
I KNEW IT!!
WATTERSON

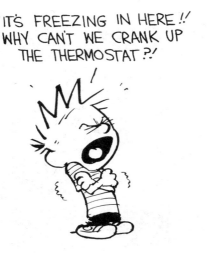

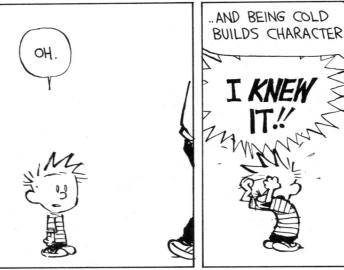

YOU'RE LISTENING TO "BOOMER 102" **CLASSIC** ROCK—WHERE WE PROMISE NOT TO EXPOSE YOU TO ANYTHING YOU HAVEN'T HEARD A MILLION TIMES BEFORE!

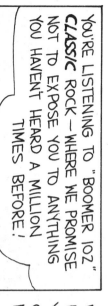

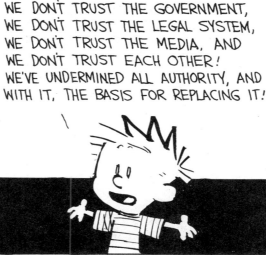

EVER NOTICE HOW MANY CONVERSATIONS REVOLVE AROUND TV SHOWS AND MOVIES?

OUR COMMON REFERENCES ARE EVENTS THAT NEVER HAPPENED AND PEOPLE WE'LL NEVER MEET! WE KNOW MORE ABOUT CELEBRITIES AND FICTIONAL CHARACTERS THAN WE KNOW ABOUT OUR NEIGHBORS!

THAT MUST BE WHY NEW HOUSES AREN'T BUILT WITH BIG FRONT PORCHES ANYMORE.
I CAN'T BELIEVE DAD WON'T LET ME HAVE A TV IN MY OWN ROOM.

I LIKE THE SOUND OF SLEET HITTING THE WINDOW PANES AT NIGHT.

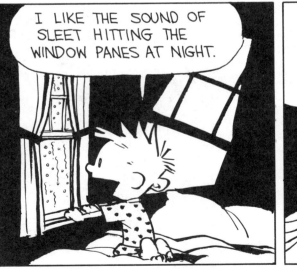

AND I LIKE WHEN THE SLEET TURNS TO HEAVY SNOW AS IT GETS COLDER, SO YOU KNOW THAT TOMORROW THE WORLD WILL BE BURIED IN ICE AND SNOW!

IT'S ONE OF THE FEW PLEASURES RESERVED FOR THOSE WHO DON'T DRIVE.

Calvin and Hobbes
by WATTERSON
SEE ANY WEIRDNESS YET?
HOW ABOUT THIS ROCK? IT HAS A PURPLE STRIPE.
HMM... I GUESS THAT'S A LITTLE WEIRD.
WE'LL LOOK FOR SOMETHING WEIRDER.

WHAT DO YOU THINK OF THIS STICK?
IT'S A STRANGE STICK, BUT IT'S NOT A WEIRD STICK.
IT'S TOO BAD THERE AREN'T ANY GOOD BUGS OUT NOW.
YES, BUGS ARE USUALLY WEIRD.
HEY, HERE'S A BIRD FEATHER.
IT'S PRETTY, BUT IT'S NOT WEIRD.
A BALD BIRD WOULD BE WEIRD.
I DON'T SEE ONE.
LOOK! A RIPPED-UP OLD KITE! SOME KID MUST HAVE LOST THIS LAST SUMMER!

PHOOEY. THE STRING BROKE HERE. I WAS HOPING WE'D FIND THE KID'S SKELETON UP A TREE AT THE OTHER END.
THAT WOULD BE WEIRD.

WELL, LET'S GO IN. I'M COLD.
ME TOO. I GUESS SOME DAYS WEIRDNESS IS HARD TO FIND.
MY GLASSES ARE FOGGED AND I CAN'T BLOW MY NOSE, BUT MY HEART RATE IS THE ENVY OF MEN HALF MY AGE!
WEIRDNESS ALWAYS STARTS AT HOME.
EVEN WHEN YOU LOOK FOR IT, YOU'RE NEVER PREPARED FOR IT.

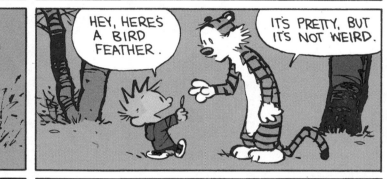

I **KNEW** I SHOULD'VE THROWN THAT SNOWBALL SOONER!

Dear Santa,
Hi, it's me, Calvin.
I have been extremely good* this year.
OBVIOUSLY, YOU'RE HOPING SANTA WON'T READ THE LONG, FINE PRINT DISCLOSURE IN THE FOOTNOTE.
I GOT THE IDEA FROM CAR ADS.

DEAR SANTA,
THIS YEAR, PLEASE BEAR IN MIND THAT I SHOULD BE PRESUMED INNOCENT UNTIL PROVEN GUILTY.

ALSO, I WOULD ENCOURAGE YOU TO INTERPRET "REASONABLE DOUBT" AS BROADLY AS POSSIBLE.

THAT'S PROBABLY A BAD WAY TO START.
WATTERSON

DO YOU THINK THERE'S AN EVIL SANTA?
AN **EVIL** SANTA??

YEAH, LIKE SANTA'S DERANGED TWIN BROTHER, OR SOMETHING! HE'D MAKE TOYS FOR ALL THE **BAD** GIRLS AND BOYS!

EVIL SANTA WOULD GIVE ALL THE DANGEROUS, ANNOYING, AND CORRUPTING TOYS YOUR PARENTS WON'T ALLOW!

AND IF YOU'RE GOOD?
HE PUNISHES YOU WITH SHIRTS AND UNDERWEAR.
WATTERSON

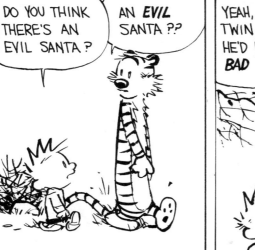

DEAR SANTA,
BEFORE I SUBMIT MY LIFE TO YOUR MORAL SCRUTINY, I DEMAND TO KNOW WHO MADE YOU THE MASTER OF MY FATE?!
WHO ARE YOU TO QUESTION MY BEHAVIOR, HUH??? WHAT GIVES YOU THE RIGHT?!

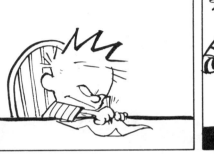

SANTA MAKES THE TOYS, SO HE GETS TO DECIDE WHO TO GIVE THEM TO.
OH.
TIME TO PREPARE MY APPELLATE CASE.

I SEE YOU, CALVIN, AND YOU'D BETTER NOT THROW THAT SNOWBALL! I'M MAILING A LETTER TO SANTA RIGHT NOW!

IS THE ENVELOPE ALREADY SEALED?
YES, BUT I COULD WRITE A P.S. ON THE BACK.
DO YOU HAVE A PEN?
AS A MATTER OF FACT, I DO!

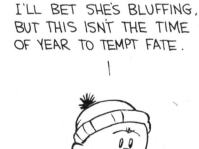

I'LL BET SHE'S BLUFFING, BUT THIS ISN'T THE TIME OF YEAR TO TEMPT FATE.

CALVIN AND HOBBES
by WATTERSON
POW!
DID YOU THROW THAT SNOWBALL AT ME ?!
WHAT SNOWBALL?
OHHHH, DON'T PLAY INNOCENT WITH ME, BUSTER! THAT SNOWBALL HAD YOUR NAME WRITTEN ALLLLL OVER IT!
OH YEAH ?!
YEAH! IT WAS SNEAKY, FIENDISH, VICIOUS, TREACHEROUS, GRIM, AND RUTHLESS! PUT ALL THAT TOGETHER AND IT SPELLS "TIGER"!
NO IT DOESN'T! IT SPELLS "CALVIN'S NEW NAME IS MR. STUPID SOGGYSHORTS!"
OOH, THAT DOES IT!
OW!
STOP THAT!
HEY!
LEGGO!
QUIT IT!
NO FAIR!
NO BITING!
HEY CALVIN, YOU SHOULD'VE SEEN YOUR EXPRESSION WHEN I HIT YOU WITH THAT SNOWBALL! HA HA!
..AH HEHH...

THERE'S A TREE! HIT THE BRAKES!
TREES **ARE** MY BRAKES.
WATTERSON

I HAVE 200 SNOWBALLS! I AM UTTERLY INVINCIBLE!
I CAN ACT WITH TOTAL IMPUNITY! I CAN DO WHATEVER I WANT!
SO JUST HANG ON WHILE I DECIDE WHAT THAT IS!
WATTERSON

WITH 200 SNOWBALLS AT MY IMMEDIATE DISPOSAL, I HAVE NO OPPOSITION! MY WILL IS LAW! I AM OMNIPOTENT!

HOW BORING.

IN THE **SHORT** TERM, IT WOULD MAKE ME HAPPY TO GO PLAY OUTSIDE.

IN THE **LONG** TERM, IT WOULD MAKE ME HAPPIER TO DO WELL AT SCHOOL AND BECOME SUCCESSFUL.

BUT IN THE **VERY** LONG TERM, I KNOW WHICH WILL MAKE BETTER MEMORIES.

FIRST SHE SAYS GO OUT. NOW SHE SAYS COME IN.
WATTERSON

HA! WHAT A ROTTEN SNOWMAN! THAT'S THE WORST SNOWMAN I'VE EVER SEEN!
SO GO BUILD A BETTER ONE!
MAYBE I WILL!
YOU'RE BACK?
MY WORDS SPEAK LOUDER THAN ACTIONS.
WATTERSON

LET'S TRY THIS PATH OVER HERE!
I DON'T SEE A PATH.

CALVIN AND HOBBES by WATTERSON
WE'LL MAKE A PATH!
HUH BOY.

CHANGE IS INVIGORATING! IF YOU DON'T ACCEPT NEW CHALLENGES, YOU BECOME COMPLACENT AND LAZY! YOUR LIFE ATROPHIES!

NEW EXPERIENCES LEAD TO NEW QUESTIONS AND NEW SOLUTIONS! CHANGE FORCES US TO EXPERIMENT AND ADAPT! THAT'S HOW WE LEARN AND GROW!

WHOOPS.. WELL, HERE'S A FRESH CHALLENGE.
I'LL ADMIT IT'S OPENED UP NEW HORIZONS.
THE PROBLEM WITH NEW EXPERIENCES IS THAT THEY'RE SO RARELY THE ONES YOU CHOOSE.
I FEEL SMARTER ALREADY.

THE CHRISTMAS SEASON IS ALWAYS A TIME FOR PERSONAL REFLECTION.

TOO OFTEN WE DON'T EXAMINE OUR LIVES. THIS IS A TIME TO TAKE STOCK AND THINK ABOUT WHAT'S IMPORTANT.

IT'S A TIME TO REDEDICATE ONESELF TO FRENZIED ACQUISITION ... A TIME TO SPREAD THE JOY OF MATERIAL WEALTH ... A TIME TO GLORIFY PERSONAL EXCESS OF EVERY KIND!
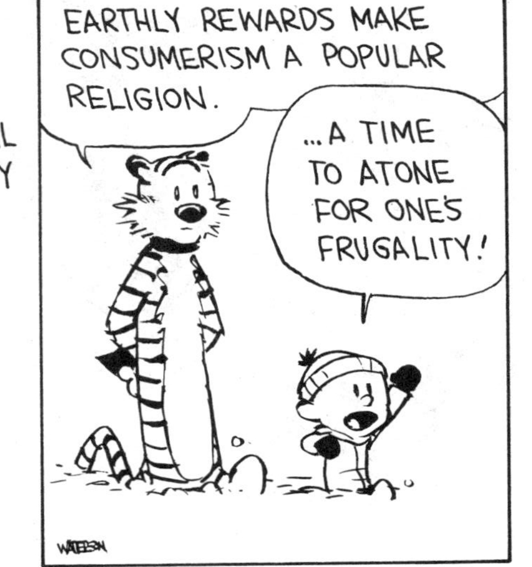
EARTHLY REWARDS MAKE CONSUMERISM A POPULAR RELIGION.
... A TIME TO ATONE FOR ONE'S FRUGALITY!

OH BOY, LOOK AT ALL THE SNOW! IT MUST BE SIX INCHES DEEP!

THIS WILL BE PERFECT FOR SLEDDING OR ...
DING DONG

DING DONG DING DONG
ALL RIGHT! I'M COMING! I'M COMING!
WHAT THE HECK IS WRONG WITH THIS PLANET YOU SOLD US?!

GALAXOID AND NEBULAR!
THIS COLD WHITE GLOP COVERS US AND FREEZES OUR INNARDS!

IT'S SNOW. YOU'D BETTER GET USED TO IT, 'CAUSE WE GET IT EVERY WINTER.
YOU DID NOT TELL US THAT THIS PLANET'S AXIS WOULD TILT US AWAY FROM THE SUN.

YOU DIDN'T ASK.
WE PAID 50 LEAVES FOR THIS PLANET! YOU GREATLY OVERCHARGED US!

YEAH WELL, "LET THE BUYER BEWARE."
YOU ARE A MOST DISHONORABLE POTENTATE!
WE DEMAND YOU BRING THIS PLANET UP TO CODE!

WHO'S AT THE DOOR, CALVIN?
AAHH! UM..UH.. GIRL SCOUTS! DO WE WANT ANY COOKIES?
GIRL SCOUTS? COOKIES?

IT SEEMS EARLY, BUT SURE, LET ME GET MY PURSE.
OH NO! SCRAM, YOU GUYS!
NOT UNTIL YOU FIX THE CLIMATE!

I'LL SEE WHAT I CAN DO.
SLAM
DO NOT TRIFLE WITH US, EARTH LEADER!

WHERE ARE THE GIRL SCOUTS?
THEY SUDDENLY HAD TO GO EARN A MERIT BADGE. QUICK, WHERE'S HOBBES?

THE ALIENS DIDN'T KNOW ABOUT WINTER?
THEY CLAIM I SOLD THEM A PLANET WITH A FAULTY AXIS! WHAT SHOULD I DO?
OFFER A REFUND. GIVE BACK THEIR LEAF COLLECTION.
ARRGGH! I THREW IT AWAY WHEN IT GOT SUCH A BAD GRADE!
HMM... WELL, WE SHOULD AT LEAST HELP THEM STAY WARM THEN.
BUT WHAT COULD THEY WEAR? THEY DON'T EVEN HAVE ARMS! ..THEY NEED HUGE SOCKS OR SOMETHING!
HEY! NO! BAD IDEA! BAD IDEA!
Hobbes
WATTERSON

OOH, THIS IS TOASTY!
THANK YOU, EARTH LEADER!
THAT'S MY CHRISTMAS STOCKING!
Calvin
Hobbes
WATTERSON
THEY'RE GOING AWAY WITH OUR STOCKINGS! SANTA CAN'T FILL 'EM WITH LOOT!
I'M SURE SANTA KNOWS WE DID A NICE THING AND HE'LL WORK IT ALL OUT.
HEY YEAH, I DID SOMETHING GOOD! WE'RE TALKING JACKPOT! WE'RE TALKING MULTIPLE TRIPS FROM THE POLE TO HAUL IT ALL!
YOUR SELFLESSNESS IS THE HOPE OF THE SEASON.

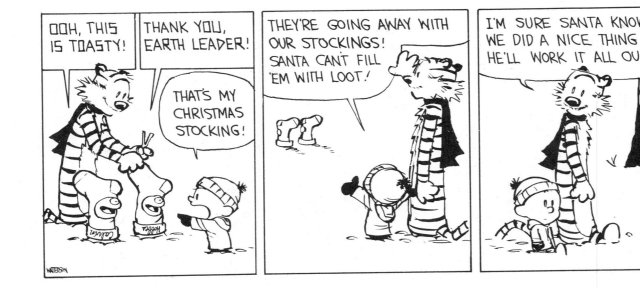

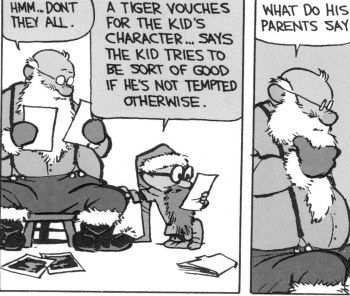

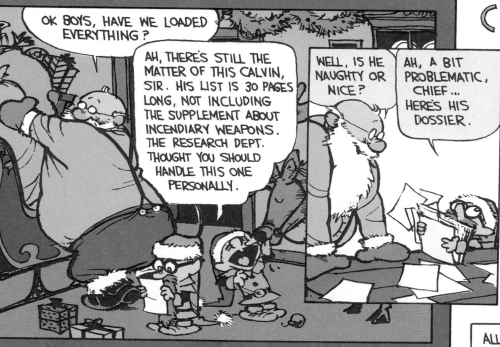

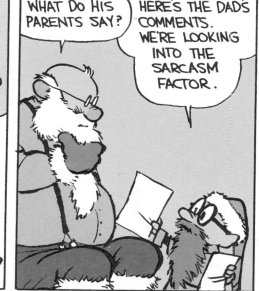

Calvin and Hobbes by WATTERSON

OK BOYS, HAVE WE LOADED EVERYTHING?
AH, THERE'S STILL THE MATTER OF THIS CALVIN, SIR. HIS LIST IS 30 PAGES LONG, NOT INCLUDING THE SUPPLEMENT ABOUT INCENDIARY WEAPONS. THE RESEARCH DEPT. THOUGHT YOU SHOULD HANDLE THIS ONE PERSONALLY.

HMM.. DONT THEY ALL.
A TIGER VOUCHES FOR THE KID'S CHARACTER... SAYS THE KID TRIES TO BE SORT OF GOOD IF HE'S NOT TEMPTED OTHERWISE.

WHAT DO HIS PARENTS SAY?
HERE'S THE DAD'S COMMENTS. WE'RE LOOKING INTO THE SARCASM FACTOR.

YOU SAY MY PRESENT FROM YOU IS OUTSIDE?
IT'S OVER HERE.
A PILE OF READY-MADE SNOWBALLS!
I WANTED TO GIVE YOU SOMETHING PRACTICAL.
FOR CALVIN
YOU'RE THE BEST, HOBBES, OL' BUDDY! THANKS!
MERRY CHRISTMAS.
I SUPPOSE IT WOULD BE WRONG TO THROW THESE AT **YOU**...
I MADE MY OWN PILE, JUST IN CASE.
FOR CALVIN
WATERSON

WHAT'S THIS?
A GENERIC SNOWMAN.
I USED TO MAKE ORIGINAL SNOWMEN, BUT IT WAS TIME-CONSUMING, HARD WORK, SO I SAID, HECK, THIS IS CRAZY!
NOW I CRANK OUT CRUDE IMITATIONS OF WHAT'S ALREADY POPULAR! IT TAKES NO TIME OR THOUGHT, AND MOST PEOPLE DON'T CARE ABOUT THE DIFFERENCE ANYWAY!
SO CYNICAL, YET SO PRACTICAL.
AND WHAT GOOD IS ORIGINALITY IF YOU CAN'T CRANK IT OUT?
WATERSON

THE NEW ISSUE OF *CHEWING* TELLS HOW TO STAY IN TOP CHEWING CONDITION OVER THE WINTER!

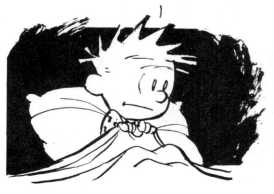

WHAT'S SO HARD ABOUT THAT? YOU CAN CHEW GUM ALL YEAR.

WE SERIOUS CHEWERS NEED A LOT MORE THAN STRONG JAW MUSCLES, YOU KNOW! TO CHEW HOUR AFTER HOUR, WE NEED A TOTAL CROSS-TRAINING FITNESS REGIME!
SO THE IDEA IS TO INCREASE THE AMOUNT OF THIS HOBBY YOU CAN ENDURE.
RIGHT. WHEN YOU'RE GOOD AT IT, IT'S REALLY MISERABLE.

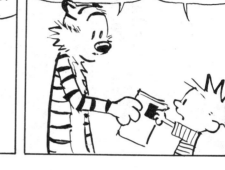

SOMETIMES AT NIGHT I WORRY ABOUT THINGS AND THEN I CAN'T FALL ASLEEP.

IN THE DARK, IT'S EASIER TO IMAGINE AWFUL POSSIBILITIES THAT YOU'D NEVER BE PREPARED FOR.

AND IT'S HARD TO FEEL COURAGEOUS IN LOOSE-FITTING, DROWSY BEAR JAMMIES.
THAT'S WHY TIGERS SLEEP IN THE BUFF!

SEE MY SNOWMAN?
HE'S ENJOYING A SNOW CONE! THERE'S NOTHING HE LIKES BETTER!
AND THE SNOWMAN WITH THE ICE CREAM SCOOP IN HIS BACK?
IT'S A SORDID STORY.

ARE YOU MAKING ANY RESOLUTIONS FOR THE NEW YEAR?
YEAH, I'M RESOLVING TO JUST WING IT AND SEE WHAT HAPPENS.
SO YOU'RE STAYING THE COURSE?
I STICK TO MY STRENGTHS.

Calvin and Hobbes
by WATTERSON
WOW, IT REALLY SNOWED LAST NIGHT! ISN'T IT WONDERFUL?
EVERYTHING FAMILIAR HAS DISAPPEARED! THE WORLD LOOKS BRAND-NEW!
A NEW YEAR... A FRESH, CLEAN START!

IT'S LIKE HAVING A BIG WHITE SHEET OF PAPER TO DRAW ON!
A DAY FULL OF POSSIBILITIES!

IT'S A MAGICAL WORLD, HOBBES, OL' BUDDY...
...LET'S GO EXPLORING!